THE ART OF TYPING
POWERFUL TOOLS FOR ENNEAGRAM TYPING

BY **GINGER LAPID-BOGDA PHD**
ILLUSTRATIONS BY **SUENAON**

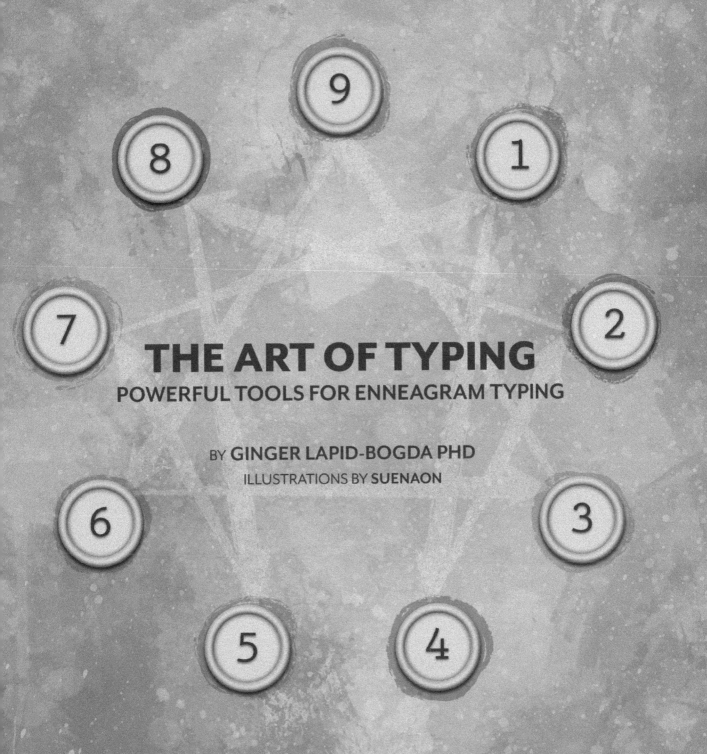

THE ART OF TYPING

POWERFUL TOOLS FOR ENNEAGRAM TYPING

BY **GINGER LAPID-BOGDA PHD**

ILLUSTRATIONS BY **SUENAON**

The Art of Typing
Powerful tools for Enneagram typing

ISBN: 978-0-9963447-7-7

The Enneagram In Business Press
Santa Monica, California
310.829.3309

www.TheEnneagramInBusiness.com

This book is dedicated to three late Enneagram teachers

Don Riso, who was passionate about
people getting their type right

Elizabeth Wagele, who introduced humor
and graphical charm to the Enneagram

David Daniels, who was instrumental
in legitimizing the Enneagram

TABLE OF CONTENTS

ACKNOWLEDGMENTS

Almost every book has many people behind it, and so has this one. The first person is Matt Ahrens, my friend, co-consultant, an Enneagram teacher and a therapist who, on the way to the memorial service for David Daniels said, "You have to turn these type differentiating blogs into a book. It would be so much more useful as a book and add other factors to it like verbal and non-verbal cues and more." And so I did, and without Matt, I doubt this book would have been written.

Next, the talented graphic artist Noa-Neus Fuentes Romero, who prior to working in my office had never heard of the Enneagram, is now Enneagram-fluent, as can be seen in her delightful illustrations throughout the book. Noa-Neus goes by the professional name Suenaon, which is Noa-Neus spelled backwards. My son, Tres Bogda, who has known the Enneagram since the age of 6 and is now 26, assisted me with the concepts for the graphics in the book and copy-edited the entire body of the book for accuracy, clarity and missing words until the final version was complete. Shelley Sakoda, The Enneagram in Business operations manager, did the final book edits. No extra spaces get past her watchful eyes.

Then, there are other Enneagram professionals who have left their mark on this book. I am forever thankful to Helen Palmer as my first Enneagram teacher, Don Riso for his friendship that I feel to this day even though he is no longer on the planet, and Claudio Naranjo, without whom the contemporary Enneagram would not be flourishing and from whom I learned the 27 Enneagram subtypes.

Next, I am deeply appreciative of the following people who gave me their insights on typing that are included on the back cover and in Chapter 4: Matt Ahrens, Andrea Isaacs, Peter O'Hanrahan, Anne Mureé, Judith Searle, Tracy Tresidder, Jerry Wagner, and Monirah Womack. In addition, Jerry was helpful in giving us thoughtful feedback on the graphical representations of the 27 Enneagram subtypes in Chapter 1.

Finally, my gratitude for the 70+ members of the global Enneagram in Business Network (EIBN), who stay engaged and make vast contributions to the Enneagram's use in organizations. They are part of my inspiration for writing this book, starting with their commitment to always getting better at assisting others in finding their Enneagram types accurately. With accurate typing, organizations, teams and people – from individual contributors to high level leaders – can use the system to create empowered, conscious, and sustainable organizations.

INTRODUCTION

WHY I WROTE THIS BOOK AND HOW TO USE IT

The single most challenging aspect of teaching the Enneagram is to assist others in discovering their Enneagram type in an accurate and respectful way. This is what I've found after more than 20 years teaching the Enneagram to the over 2000 trainers, coaches and consultants I've trained to teach others the Enneagram, but also from my direct work with thousands of individuals within organizations.

When someone is brand new to the Enneagram, it is often easier to help them learn the Enneagram system and discover their types accurately than someone who has known the Enneagram for a while and been mistyped. Usually I can help people type themselves in group settings and within 3-4 hours, about 75-80% of the group can find their types accurately; the remaining 20-25% may take longer. Over the years, I have developed effective and efficient ways to help people type themselves, including asking people insightful differentiating questions – but only after they have narrowed down their search to two possible types. Narrowing the possibilities to two types comes, of course, after teaching the system and the nine types using slides and stories, graphics and Enneagram typing cards or other tools.

When someone has been mistyped and they have come to identify with being that particular type, it can be very difficult for them to consider other possibilities. Sometimes a teacher, someone they respect, has told them they were a certain type, so to reconsider type is to challenge this teacher's expertise and even cause tension in the relationship if the mistyped individual maintains an ongoing relationship with that teacher.

Others can be mistyped because they took an Enneagram test that indicated they were a certain type that wasn't accurate, and they believed the test results. These individuals don't realize that Enneagram tests are indicators, but are not necessarily definitive, and some tests, of course, are better than others at getting type accurately.

Another cause of mistyping is that someone has read an Enneagram book, read the nine type descriptions, and has then identified his or her type incorrectly. Some books are more accurate than others or readers can misinterpret some of the book's key words and phrases. This happens all the time.

Finally, the Enneagram system is complex and can take people some time and self-reflection to figure out which type truly describes them best. Add to this additional Enneagram dimensions such as arrows and wings, subtypes, Centers of Intelligence, Levels of Development or self-mastery, and "look alikes" – types that have some similar characteristics but only on the surface – and getting your type right becomes more complicated. Finally, there are "want-to-be" individuals, those who want to think of themselves in a specific way that aligns more with a certain type, yet that is really not how they are at all. This often goes with lack of self-awareness; "getting type right" requires reasonably self-aware individuals.

Why accurate typing is so important

Discovering type supports accurate self-observation
Mistyped people pay attention to the wrong things

Deep psychological and spiritual development is directly connected to type
Wrong type means the wrong development path

Relationships with others improve from knowing your type and theirs
Mistyped people misunderstand or misinterpret their own impact on others

Almost all applications of the Enneagram require accurate type identification
Improving leadership style, teams, interactions, conflict and coaching, just as examples, all require that people know their types

People need to have themselves typed accurately to teach type to others
Minimally, mistyped teachers typically teach two types incorrectly: the teacher's real type and the type they think they are

Why I wrote this book

I wrote this book to help others type themselves and others in a more accurate way. It is not intended to teach or share everything I know about the Enneagram system or the nine types; it is specifically about how to respectfully, intelligently and consciously help ourselves and others uncover our Enneagram types more accurately.

This book is also about encouraging us to not tell someone else what his or her type is, even if we think we know it. It is about the nuances of each type, hopefully to minimize unintentional stereotyping or one-factor typing – for example, communication style or posture – when teaching the nine types. It is about identifying type based on a person's Ego structure and not behavior because several types can do the same thing but for very different reasons. It is about moving beyond our own value judgments about types – for example, healthy versus unhealthy or good types versus bad types – and the words we choose when describing each type. Words matter; they reflect what we think, and they have power.

The Enneagram is also a sacred system, one that has passed through centuries and generations, evolving over time and offering greater and greater clarity about ourselves, others, processes, and consciousness at an individual and a collective level.

As such, the Enneagram is precious but not fragile. As honored Enneagram teacher Don Riso, who was also a dear friend, used to say to me, "Ginger, don't be worried about how the Enneagram is being used. The Enneagram is bigger than all of us." Still, I want to do my part in helping the world find and use this incredible system in the best of ways.

How to use this book

This book is divided into three parts, plus an appendix and a resources section.

Part I provides the foundation of understanding. Chapter 1, "What is Enneagram type?," provides a robust explanation, both logical and visual, that type is neither personality nor character – Enneagram type is nine versions of the Ego structure. Chapter 2, "Getting type right," contains real stories explaining why getting type right matters and the various ways people can get it wrong.

Part II, Chapter 3, "Differentiating questions," is the heart of the book, providing differentiating questions you can ask others to help them clarify their type and, specifically, to distinguish between two types. In addition to three questions to ask and what to listen for when the person answers, there are illustrations that metaphorically illustrate how the two types might do the very same activity very differently.

Part III, Chapter 4, "Other typing factors," includes other factors to consider when uncovering Enneagram type, such as a person's current context; overlays on type related to a person's family, culture, gender, and more; a person's level of self-mastery; wing and arrow usage; and verbal and nonverbal typing cues, with insights from experienced Enneagram teachers.

The Appendix is like a real appendix; you might or might not need it as you engage in typing! This includes more information on the following:

Teaching Type (Appendix A)

3 Centers of Intelligence (Appendix B)

Wings and Arrows (Appendix C)

27 Enneagram Subtypes (Appendix D)

Enneagram Triads (Appendix E)

Finally, there is a section with Additional Resources that includes information on books, websites, tests, apps, training tools and typing-related training programs that are particularly useful for guidance in accurate typing.

I hope this book makes a contribution to all of us who hold the Enneagram with honor, respect and compassion.

Ginger.

CHAPTER 1 | WHAT IS ENNEAGRAM TYPE?

The Enneagram is a psychological and spiritual system that goes beyond the personality into a deep and powerful description of the nine human architectures, specifically the nine structures of the Ego. The Enneagram's Asian and Middle Eastern roots are 2000 - 4000 years old, and part of its foundation comes from the Eastern practice of self-observation: the objective observation of the pattern of one's thoughts, feelings, somatic experiences and behaviors.

The word Enneagram comes from the Greek words *ennea* or "nine" and *gram* or "something written or drawn" and refers to the nine points on the Enneagram symbol. These nine different Enneagram types or points are connected to a specific and unique path of development.

A person's Enneagram type appears early in childhood and does not change over time, although individuals of the same type may behave quite differently based on a number of factors: level of self-mastery; use of wings – the types on either side of a person's core Enneagram type; use of arrow lines – the arrow lines pointing toward and away from the individual's core type; and subtypes, the three different versions of each type. To support others in the discovery of their type, it is essential for the guide to understand the Enneagram system and what Enneagram type is and is not.

IS THE ENNEAGRAM *PERSONALITY, CHARACTER* OR *EGO STRUCTURE*?

The Enneagram, a profound way of understanding people from all cultures, describes the nine fundamental architectures of human beings. Although the Enneagram is often referred to as a personality system, it is far more than that. The Enneagram is also more than character structure. Both personality and character refer to persistent features of human behavior; the nine Enneagram types represent nine distinct aspects of the human Ego.

WHAT IS *PERSONALITY*?

Personality exists in the domain of empirical psychology – that is, research and theory based in the field of applied psychology – and as such, personality represents a set of traits and behaviors capable of being measured. For example, traits and behaviors such as introversion, ambition, agreeableness and sociability can be both observed and, with some degree of objectivity, measured.

The nine Enneagram types are not nine sets of distinct traits or behaviors. In fact, several Enneagram types may have some similar traits and behaviors – for example, being hardworking or being sociable-relational – but the particular ways in which they demonstrate these traits and, more importantly, the motivations driving these traits are categorically different.

WHAT IS *CHARACTER STRUCTURE*?

Character structure refers to aspects of a person that go deeper than personality and typically involves qualities to which we assign positive or negative values – for example, kind or cruel, honest or dishonest, having integrity or being deceptive. Character falls more into the domain of philosophy, qualities of the inner life that have a moral component and are also more subjective and, therefore, harder to measure.

The Enneagram is closer to character structure than personality, but the Enneagram types are not character in the sense described above. In general, each Enneagram type has positive and negative qualities. However, positive and negative qualities do not mean good or bad in a moral sense; they are simply aspects of a person that they and others may like or dislike or that support or hinder them. In addition, the positive and negative characteristics have specific meanings related to that type; the meaning of the characteristics can only be accurately understood in the entire construct for that type.

As an example, Enneagram 3s are described as "deceitful," but this does not mean that they chronically lie or that they are more deceptive than the other Enneagram types. Deceit, in this context, refers to how Enneagram 3s hide parts of themselves from themselves, as well as others, and that these hidden parts are qualities that do not conform to the 3's self-image as a successful, competent, and capable person. Taken in context, "deceit" for 3s is more about self-deception or not being honest with oneself, although it does impact what they share with others.

WHAT IS *EGO STRUCTURE?*

The term "Ego" has many definitions, but the one applicable to the Enneagram derives from both Freudian psychology and spiritual traditions.

The Psychological Ego

From the Freudian psychological perspective, the Ego navigates between the Id, or unconscious impulses, and the Superego, the internalized societal rules and norms that hold us in check. In the Freudian sense, the Ego is the self – often defined as the rational self – in daily life. It is the individual's inner architecture, as well as how he or she interacts with and responds to the external world. The function of the Ego is even more intricate; it provides individuals with both continuity and consistency by providing a personal point of reference that connects events of the past with experiences in the present and possibilities or probabilities of the future. The past is accessed through subjective memories, the future through anticipation and imagination, with the Ego linking all three elements together. A person's Ego-ideal is part of the Ego, but refers specifically to how a person most wants to perceive him- or herself, even if true reality doesn't quite match.

The Spiritual Meaning Of Ego

The Ego, from a spiritual perspective, is the over-identification with what you perceive as self and a specific over-identification with your thoughts and thought patterns, emotions and emotional response patterns, and behavior and behavioral patterns. Another word for identification is attachment, and this refers to being attached to your self-perception, your thoughts, feelings and behaviors as if these are all of who you are when, in fact, your truest self or essence goes far deeper. From a spiritual perspective, the path to greater consciousness is to increasingly dis-identify from or lessen one's attachment to the Ego.

Each of the nine Enneagram types has its own Ego structure. Each aspect of this structure is important for typing oneself accurately and guiding others. Also significant is the connection between each type's unique spiritual attunement and how the type-based Ego structure directly blocks access to this particular spiritual dimension. The generic Ego structure description on these two pages is followed by the Ego structures for the nine Enneagram types.

PSYCHOLOGICAL EGO STRUCTURE

FALSE REALITY

The pervasive, but mistaken, veil or screen used for interpreting what occurs internally and externally

WORLDVIEW

An unexamined perspective on how the world operates and how to function within it that seeks to get continuously reaffirmed

EGO IDEAL

How a person wants to be perceived by self and others that seeks to be continuously reinforced – defined as *me* – and when this does not occur, the *not-me* then gets projected onto others*

DEEPEST UNMET LONGING

What a person most deeply desires that never seems to get fully satisfied

THIRST AND AVOIDANCE

Areas, often unconscious, that become habitual driving forces, propelling us toward something and away from something else

PRIMARY DEFENSE MECHANISM HOLDING THE EGO STRUCTURE IN PLACE

The first line of psychological defense against uncomfortable feelings, thoughts, and behaviors that also protects the Ego and holds it in place; if these defenses prove insufficient, additional defense mechanisms arise

*from the work of Jerry Wagner PhD in "Nine Lenses on the World"

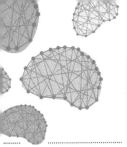
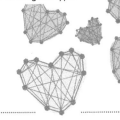

THOUGHT PATTERN	EMOTIONAL PATTERN
The patterns of thought that are continuously playing in our minds, commonly referred to as the Enneagram type *fixation*	The patterns of feeling that are persistent and fuel our emotional reactions, commonly referred to as the Enneagram type *passion* or *vice*

BEHAVIORAL PATTERN | 3 SUBTYPE VARIATIONS

Our repeated behavioral patterns are related to our subtype, one of three versions of each type. Subtypes are formed when the emotional pattern for each type – the *passion* or *vice* – intersects with one of the three basic human instincts that is most active in us (and we may have more than one active instinct): self-preservation, social, and one-to-one. Each instinct has focal areas; individuals with that active instinct may move toward, away from, or have ambivalence about these areas.

Self-preservation instinct focal areas	Social instinct focal areas	One-to-one instinct focal areas
physical comfort	belonging	self with one other
safety	community	affection
security	groups	intimacy
danger	social relationships	bonding
resources	influence	attraction
structure	support	1-1 relationships

HOW THE *EGO STRUCTURE* INTERFERES WITH SPIRITUAL DIMENSION OF TYPE

Spiritual Dimension

Each Enneagram type is particularly attuned to one spiritual dimension that they long for, but can't seem to access easily. These are connected to the higher states for each type: the *holy idea* for the Mental Center and the *virtue* for the Emotional Center.

Psychological Ego Structure Interference

The Ego structure generates repeated responses that are attempts to access the spiritual dimension to which the person is attuned; paradoxically, this attempt takes the person in the opposite direction.

Type ONE

Want a more perfect world and work relentlessly to improve themselves, others, and everything around them; are highly self-controlled and structured; strive for 100% excellence; believe that there is almost always a right way to do everything

PSYCHOLOGICAL EGO STRUCTURE

FALSE REALITY

False Impeccability

WORLDVIEW

The world is imperfect; I must correct this

THIRST AND AVOIDANCE

Thirst for perfection; avoid mistakes

EGO IDEAL

The Good Person
Always moral and responsible; never bad or mediocre*

DEEPEST UNMET LONGING

To experience a tranquil life, accepting the world as it is

PRIMARY DEFENSE MECHANISM HOLDING THE EGO STRUCTURE IN PLACE

Reaction Formation
Trying to reduce or eliminate their anxiety caused by their own thoughts, feelings, or behaviors that they consider unacceptable by responding in a manner that is the exact opposite of their true response, all without recognizing this

*from the work of Jerry Wagner PhD in "Nine Lenses on the World"

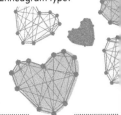

THOUGHT PATTERN	EMOTIONAL PATTERN
Resentment | Noticing how everything is flawed	*Anger* | Chronic anger and dissatisfaction with how things are

BEHAVIORAL PATTERN | 3 SUBTYPE VARIATIONS

Self-preservation **Subtype One**	Social **Subtype One**	One-to-one **Subtype One**
"WORRY"	**"NON-ADAPTABILITY"**	**"ZEAL"**
Highly self-controlled and focus on getting everything correctly structured and organized, wanting to make sure everything is under control, and feeling both anxious, irritated or frustrated (angry) until they can ensure that everything is being done right *Can be confused with a 6 or self-preservation subtype 3*	Perceive themselves as the perfect role model for others to emulate, becoming angry when others do not meet their standards, and focusing their anger on social institutions as a way to perfect them	Intense need to perfect others, particularly those who matter to them, and to perfect society in general, perceiving reforming others as both their right and responsibility *Can be confused with one-to-one subtype 8*

HOW THE *EGO STRUCTURE* INTERFERES WITH SPIRITUAL DIMENSION OF TYPE

Spiritual Dimension

Holy Perfection

Knowing that everything is *perfection* just as it is, including imperfections, combined with *serenity*, an open-hearted acceptance of all that occurs

Psychological Ego Structure Interference

Trying to correct and perfect everyone and everything in the everyday world

Type TWO

Want to be liked by those who are in need, by important people, and by those who are important to them; attempt to feel worthy and valued by offering gifts, attention, resources and advice to others; lose connection with what they themselves truly want and deeply need

PSYCHOLOGICAL EGO STRUCTURE

FALSE REALITY

False Abundance

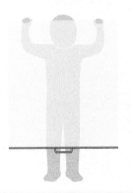

WORLDVIEW

The world is full of suffering and need; I must help alleviate this

EGO IDEAL

The Loving Person
Always thoughtful and generous; never selfish or insensitive*

THIRST AND AVOIDANCE

Thirst for appreciation; avoid feeling unworthy

DEEPEST UNMET LONGING

To feel a deep and firm sense of self-worth that is not dependent on how others respond

PRIMARY DEFENSE MECHANISM HOLDING THE EGO STRUCTURE IN PLACE

Repression
Hiding information from themselves and others – for example, feelings, thoughts, desires, and needs – through unconscious, partial suppression, thus keeping it contained and under control

*from the work of Jerry Wagner PhD in "Nine Lenses on the World"

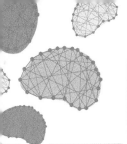

THOUGHT PATTERN	EMOTIONAL PATTERN
Flattery | Gaining acceptance through giving compliments or other forms of attention	*Pride* | Inflated or deflated self-esteem based on doing for other people and the subsequent positive or negative reactions of others

BEHAVIORAL PATTERN | 3 SUBTYPE VARIATIONS

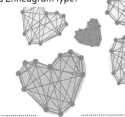

Self-preservation **Subtype Two**
"ME-FIRST/ PRIVILEGE"

Deny own needs for protection, while trying to attract others for protection; appear to be without guile, even childlike; ambivalent about closeness and trust; as Enneagram royalty, they are princes and princesses, giving up the rights of an adult for the privileges of a child *Can be confused with self-preservation subtype 6*

Social **Subtype Two**
"AMBITION"

Focus on helping groups as a way to stand above the group without acknowledging this; intellectually oriented; comfortable in visibly powerful positions; as Enneagram royalty, they are emperors and empresses, having to continually earn their territory *Can be confused with social subtype 8*

One-to-one **Subtype Two**
"AGGRESSION/ SEDUCTION"

Oriented to individual relationships and meeting the needs of important people as a way to get their own needs met, becoming angry if this does not occur; as Enneagram royalty, they are kings and queens, with royalty as their birthright *Can be confused with one-to-one subtype 4*

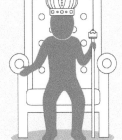

HOW THE *EGO STRUCTURE* INTERFERES WITH SPIRITUAL DIMENSION OF TYPE

Spiritual Dimension
Holy Will and Holy Freedom
Knowing that *free will* comes from acknowledging oneself and one's own needs, combined with *humility*, or true self-acceptance without deference to the reactions of others

Psychological Ego Structure Interference
Trying to find self-worth externally, based on the approval of others for good deeds done, and perceiving self as independent when, in fact, there is extreme dependency on the reactions of others

Type THREE

Want respect from others for being successful and worthy of admiration through focusing intensely on specific goals and plans, all with a self-assured and confident demeanor and image; become out of touch with their truest self and innermost heart's desire

PSYCHOLOGICAL EGO STRUCTURE

FALSE REALITY

False Manifestation

WORLDVIEW

There is a lack of order and flow to how things work; I must organize and plan to make things happen and get results

EGO IDEAL

The Effective Person
Always professional and competent; never idle or inadequate*

THIRST AND AVOIDANCE

Thirst for success and respect; avoid failure

DEEPEST UNMET LONGING

To know who they really are and to be valued by both themselves and others for who they are, not just what they accomplish

PRIMARY DEFENSE MECHANISM HOLDING THE EGO STRUCTURE IN PLACE

Identification
Over-identifying with activities, roles, or work and also incorporating attributes of other admirable people into self to such an extent that the self and the admired others become indistinguishable

*from the work of Jerry Wagner PhD in "Nine Lenses on the World"

THOUGHT PATTERN	EMOTIONAL PATTERN

Vanity | Strategic thinking about how to create an idealized image based on being or appearing to be successful

Deceit | Feeling you must do everything possible to appear confident and successful, hiding parts of yourself that do not conform to this image

BEHAVIORAL PATTERN | 3 SUBTYPE VARIATIONS

Self-preservation **Subtype Three**
"SECURITY"

Need to be seen as a good or ideal person who is self-reliant, autonomous, hardworking, with an image of having no image and needing the security of structure to avoid fear of failure
Can be confused with a 6 or self-preservation subtype 1

Social **Subtype Three**
"PRESTIGE"

Need to be seen as successful and admirable in the context of specific social reference groups; like being around other successful people because proximity reinforces their own image and status
Can be confused with a 7

One-to-one **Subtype Three**
"MASCULINITY/ FEMININITY"

Need to be seen as attractive in a masculine or feminine way, as well as successful, by individuals who are important to them and whom they want to attract; also help these others achieve success *Can be confused with one-to-one subtype 2*

HOW THE *EGO STRUCTURE* INTERFERES WITH SPIRITUAL DIMENSION OF TYPE

Spiritual Dimension
Holy Law
Knowing that through *hope*, you can have faith that there is a natural rhythm to everything that occurs without any effort on your part and that through *truthfulness*, you can find self-acceptance and be valued for who you truly are

Psychological Ego Structure Interference
Trying to constantly create goals, plans and results, then attempting to find your value through what you accomplish rather than who you are

Type FOUR

Want a deep, unbreakable and authentic relationship with themselves and others; pursue meaning, symbolism, and aesthetics as a way to understand and express the perplexing puzzle of human suffering; try to understand why they feel so different from everyone else

PSYCHOLOGICAL EGO STRUCTURE

FALSE REALITY

False Deficiency

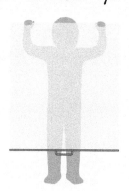

WORLDVIEW

There is a profound despair that comes from our lack of deep connections; I must re-establish these

EGO IDEAL

The Original Person
Always creative and authentic; never ordinary or boring*

THIRST AND AVOIDANCE

Thirst for deep feelings and connections with others; avoid rejection and feeling not good enough

DEEPEST UNMET LONGING

To live a deep, purposeful, and emotionally balanced life

PRIMARY DEFENSE MECHANISM HOLDING THE EGO STRUCTURE IN PLACE

Introjection
Fully absorbing and internalizing negative information about themselves without discerning if the data is accurate, along with the absence of counterbalancing internalized positive data

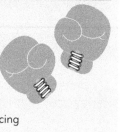

*from the work of Jerry Wagner PhD in "Nine Lenses on the World"

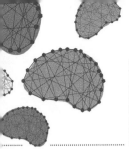
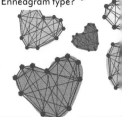

THOUGHT PATTERN	EMOTIONAL PATTERN
Melancholy | Continuously thinking about what is missing, accompanied with thoughts of being disconnected from others	*Envy* | Consciously or unconsciously comparing self to others, with accompanying feelings of deficiency, superiority, or both

BEHAVIORAL PATTERN | 3 SUBTYPE VARIATIONS

Self-preservation **Subtype Four**	Social **Subtype Four**	One-to-one **Subtype Four**
"RECKLESS/ DAUNTLESS"	**"SHAME"**	**"COMPETITION"**
Bear their suffering in silence to prove that they are good enough by virtue of enduring pain; engage in nonstop activity or reckless behavior as a way to feel excited and energized *Can be confused with a 7 or a 3*	Focus on their deficiencies and on earning understanding and appreciation for their suffering, particularly from the groups to which they belong or lead, yet they still feel marginal to these groups	Express needs and feelings outwardly and intensely, while being highly competitive in order to gain attention, to be heard, and to be acknowledged *Can be confused with one-to-one subtype 8*

HOW THE *EGO STRUCTURE* INTERFERES WITH SPIRITUAL DIMENSION OF TYPE

Spiritual Dimension
Holy Origin
Knowing that nothing is missing and that everyone and everything is deeply connected because we all emanate from the same *original source* and that emotional *equilibrium* creates clarity and balance in thought, feeling and action

Psychological Ego Structure Interference
Trying to constantly find and sustain deep connections with self and others in all aspects of everyday life, with accompanying emotional volatility when this does not occur

Type FIVE

Want to absorb knowledge in the areas they perceive as important and intriguing, becoming highly cerebral, emotionally detached, and self-contained; extraordinarily private as a way to guard against intrusion and the experience of feeling energetically depleted

PSYCHOLOGICAL EGO STRUCTURE

FALSE REALITY

False Scarcity

WORLDVIEW

Resources are scarce; I must conserve my time, energy and knowledge or I will be entirely depleted

EGO IDEAL

The Wise Person
Always knowledgeable and autonomous; never emotional or transparent*

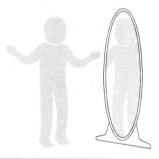

THIRST AND AVOIDANCE

Thirst for knowledge and wisdom; avoid intrusion by others and loss of energy

DEEPEST UNMET LONGING

To experience and fully understand life at all levels – mental, emotional and physical

PRIMARY DEFENSE MECHANISM HOLDING THE EGO STRUCTURE IN PLACE

Isolation
Isolating oneself, fully retreating into their minds and cutting off from their feelings and somatic experiences, separating themselves from other people, and compartmentalizing parts of themselves from other parts of themselves

*from the work of Jerry Wagner PhD in "Nine Lenses on the World"

THOUGHT PATTERN

Stinginess | A scarcity paradigm leading to an insatiable thirst for knowing, a reluctance to share and to strategizing about how to control one's environment

EMOTIONAL PATTERN

Avarice | An intense desire to guard everything related to oneself, combined with automatic detachment from feelings

BEHAVIORAL PATTERN | 3 SUBTYPE VARIATIONS

Self-preservation **Subtype Five**
"CASTLE"

Concerned with being intruded upon and being overextended physically and energetically; guard their involvement with others just as they guard their scarce resources in their own private space or "castle"

Social **Subtype Five**
"TOTEM"

Find, develop and guard strong bonds with individuals and groups who share their ideals and interests, but become disengaged when forced to live in a way that is not aligned with these higher-order beliefs

One-to-one **Subtype Five**
"CONFIDENCE"

Search for a strong, deep connection with one other person whom they trust and have confidence in and with whom they can share confidences; preserve and protect themselves, the other person, and these special relationships

HOW THE *EGO STRUCTURE* INTERFERES WITH SPIRITUAL DIMENSION OF TYPE

Spiritual Dimension
Holy Omniscience and Holy Transparency
Understanding that only through direct personal experience, complete engagement, and openness can *omniscience* be achieved and that *non-attachment* is not the same as detachment

Psychological Ego Structure Interference
Trying to constantly find wisdom through the mind alone – through accumulating data and knowledge – and mistaking detachment, which is disconnection, from non-attachment, which is being connected but also allowing that which you love to be free

Type SIX

Want to enable the best to manifest and the worst from occurring, with an elaborate scanning antenna that generates a variety of anticipatory scenarios in order to be prepared should something go wrong; may shrink from fear, go directly into fearful situations to prove their bravery, or both

PSYCHOLOGICAL EGO STRUCTURE

FALSE REALITY

False Fear

DEEPEST UNMET LONGING

To be able to fully trust themselves, others, and their environment

WORLDVIEW

The world is an unstable, unpredictable and dangerous place; I must find meaning, stability and support

THIRST AND AVOIDANCE

Thirst for meaning, certainty and trust; avoid negative scenarios from occurring

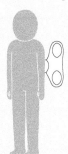

EGO IDEAL

The Loyal Person
Always reliable and consistent; never untrustworthy or difficult*

PRIMARY DEFENSE MECHANISM HOLDING THE EGO STRUCTURE IN PLACE

Projection
Unconsciously attributing their own feelings, drives, intentions, thoughts and behaviors onto other people; these externalized attributions can be positive qualities or negative qualities

*from the work of Jerry Wagner PhD in "Nine Lenses on the World"

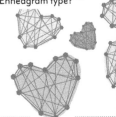

Cowardice | Thoughts of doubt and worry that cause the continuous creation of anticipatory or worse-case scenarios

Fear | Feelings of anxiety, deep concern, and panic that the worst will occur, that others cannot be trusted, and that they are not capable of meeting the challenges that present themselves

BEHAVIORAL PATTERN | 3 SUBTYPE VARIATIONS

Self-preservation **Subtype Six**

"WARMTH"

An intense need to feel protected from danger, often utilizing the family, a surrogate family or support groups to provide this; use their warmth and friendliness as a way to feel safe *Can be confused with self-preservation subtype 2*

Social **Subtype Six**

"DUTY"

Focus on following rules, regulations, and prescribed ways of behaving within social environments or groups as a way to keep their behavior acceptable and not get chastised or punished by authority figures *Can be confused with a 1*

One-to-one **Subtype Six**

"STRENGTH/ BEAUTY"

Deny their own anxieties and vulnerabilities by pushing against their fear, appearing bold, confident, charismatic and sometimes fierce or fearless *Can be confused with an 8*

HOW THE *EGO STRUCTURE* INTERFERES WITH SPIRITUAL DIMENSION OF TYPE

Spiritual Dimension
Holy Faith

The *faith* that both you and others can capably meet life's challenges and having the *courage* to overcome fear through fully conscious action and knowing that there is meaning and certainty in the world

Psychological Ego Structure Interference

Trying to constantly find courage, certainty and authority outside oneself rather than internally by seeking safety through self doubt, adhering to rules, acting strong, or taking risks to prove you are not afraid

Type SEVEN

Want to experience everything possible that is new, stimulating, exciting, and pleasurable, while rebelling against limits or restraints; have minds that move instantaneously from one thought to another, hearts that avoid sorrow, and bodies that are constantly in motion

PSYCHOLOGICAL EGO STRUCTURE

FALSE REALITY

False Freedom

DEEPEST UNMET LONGING

To feel complete, whole and solid

WORLDVIEW

The world lacks a bigger plan full of possibilities; I must generate these

THIRST AND AVOIDANCE

Thirst for stimulation and pleasure; avoid pain, discomfort and limitations

EGO IDEAL

The Joyful Person
Always optimistic and enthusiastic; never trapped or pessimistic*

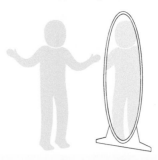

PRIMARY DEFENSE MECHANISM HOLDING THE EGO STRUCTURE IN PLACE

Rationalization
Explaining uncomfortable or unacceptable thoughts, feelings and behavior to both themselves and others in a way that deflects or obscures the true motivation, intention or impact of the behavior

*from the work of Jerry Wagner PhD in "Nine Lenses on the World"

THOUGHT PATTERN	**EMOTIONAL PATTERN**
Planning | The mental process through which the mind goes into "hyper-gear" by moving in rapid succession from one thing to another	*Gluttony* | The insatiable, unrelenting thirst for new stimulation of all kinds: food, people, experience, ideas, excitement

BEHAVIORAL PATTERN | 3 SUBTYPE VARIATIONS

Self-preservation **Subtype Seven**	Social **Subtype Seven**	One-to-one **Subtype Seven**
"KEEPERS OF THE CASTLE"	**"SACRIFICE"**	**"SUGGESTABILITY/ FASCINATION"**
Create close networks of family, friends, and colleagues to keep themselves feeling stimulated and secure, but also to generate new and interesting deals and opportunities	Sacrifice stimulation momentarily in service of the group or an important ideal by postponing their gratification, but want recognition for their sacrifice and then get what they want later *Can be confused with a 2*	Need to see the stark reality of the world through rose-colored glasses so that this embellished reality helps them live in a dream-like state; have highly idealized view of intimate relationships that rarely live up to this ideal

HOW THE *EGO STRUCTURE* INTERFERES WITH SPIRITUAL DIMENSION OF TYPE

Spiritual Dimension

Holy Work and Holy Plan

The ability to control and sustain mental focus to the *work* at hand, while feeling full and complete through the *sobriety* that comes from integrating painful and uncomfortable experiences with pleasurable and stimulating ones

Psychological Ego Structure Interference

Trying to constantly seek that which is novel and exciting while rebelling against any limitations or repetition, mistaking having no rules or limits for freedom and avoiding pain and sorrow

Type EIGHT

Want truth, justice, and situations to be under control, becoming bold and bigger than life, and perceiving things in black and white terms with little gray in between; hiding their vulnerability by taking big, immediate action

PSYCHOLOGICAL EGO STRUCTURE

FALSE REALITY

False Strength

DEEPEST UNMET LONGING

To regain their lost purity and goodness while still feeling strong and vital

WORLDVIEW

The powerful take advantage of the weak; I must change this

THIRST AND AVOIDANCE

Thirst for control and justice; avoid feeling vulnerable or weak

EGO IDEAL

The Powerful Person
Always invincible and forceful; never weak or cowardly*

PRIMARY DEFENSE MECHANISM HOLDING THE EGO STRUCTURE IN PLACE

Denial
Negating the very existence of any thoughts, feelings or behaviors that cause them anxiety or feelings of vulnerability by disavowing these emotions entirely, as if they never occurred or existed

*from the work of Jerry Wagner PhD in "Nine Lenses on the World"

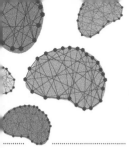

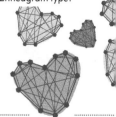

THOUGHT PATTERN	EMOTIONAL PATTERN
Vengeance | Thinking about rebalancing wrongs through thoughts about anger, blame and intimidation	*Lust* | Excessiveness in a variety of forms as a way to avoid and deny feelings of vulnerability and weakness

BEHAVIORAL PATTERN | 3 SUBTYPE VARIATIONS

Self-preservation **Subtype Eight**	Social **Subtype Eight**	One-to-one **Subtype Eight**
"SURVIVAL"	**"SOLIDARITY"**	**"POSSESSION"**
Get what they need for survival, scoping out the scene particularly related to power and influence, becoming highly frustrated, intolerant, and angry when the fulfillment of their needs is thwarted in any way	Vigorously protect others from unjust and unfair authorities and systems and challenge social norms, while seeking power, influence, and pleasure *Can be confused with social subtype 2*	Rebellious, provocative, emotional, intense, and passionate; draw others to them; get power and influence from being at the center of and controlling events and other people *Can be confused with one-to-one subtype 4 or one-to-one subtype 6*

HOW THE *EGO STRUCTURE* INTERFERES WITH SPIRITUAL DIMENSION OF TYPE

Spiritual Dimension
Holy Truth
Being able to seek and integrate multiple points of view into a higher or bigger *truth*, with a childlike *innocence* and a willingness to be vulnerable, open-minded and open-hearted so that the need to protect self and others is no longer present

Psychological Ego Structure Interference
Trying to constantly exert control and extract justice, perceiving their own instinctual reactions as the truth, while using intensity, anger and the appearance of strength to hide vulnerability

Type NINE

Want peace, harmony, and mutual positive regard; avoid conflict, and don't readily access or express their own points of view; embrace multiple perspectives; prefer a relaxed demeanor or "going along to get along" rather than to potentially create tension between themselves and others

PSYCHOLOGICAL EGO STRUCTURE

FALSE REALITY

False Harmony

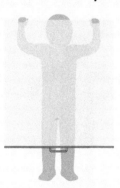

DEEPEST UNMET LONGING

To know that they matter enough to both speak their truth and take values-based action

WORLDVIEW

Everyone deserves to be respected and heard; I must enable this

THIRST AND AVOIDANCE

Thirst for harmony and comfort; avoid direct conflict and ill will

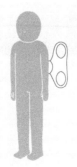

EGO IDEAL

The Peaceful Person
Always easygoing and accepting; never pushy or ambitious*

PRIMARY DEFENSE MECHANISM HOLDING THE EGO STRUCTURE IN PLACE

Narcotization
Numbing themselves to avoid uncomfortable thoughts, feelings, and behaviors, as well as difficult tasks, conflict, anger or pressure by merging with others and engaging in routines that require little attention and provide maximum comfort

*from the work of Jerry Wagner PhD in "Nine Lenses on the World"

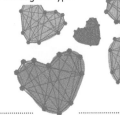

THOUGHT PATTERN	EMOTIONAL PATTERN
Indolence | Mentally diffusing attention so that you forget what is important and refrain from stating opinions and positions, thereby minimizing tensions and conflict with others	*Laziness* | A lethargy in paying attention to your own feelings, thoughts, and needs, thus disabling desired action

BEHAVIORAL PATTERN | 3 SUBTYPE VARIATIONS

Self-preservation **Subtype Nine**	Social **Subtype Nine**	One-to-one **Subtype Nine**
"APPETITE"	**"PARTICIPATION"**	**"FUSION/UNION"**
Merge with the comfort of routine and rhythmic or pleasant activities as a way to not pay attention to themselves; often have collections of multiple versions of similar items to which they have a sentimental attachment	Merge with – and work extremely hard on behalf of – a group, organization or cause that they support or belong to as a way of not focusing on themselves *Can be confused with a 3*	Merge with one other person – or a series of others – as a way of not paying attention to their own thoughts, feelings, needs, and desires *Can be confused with a 2*

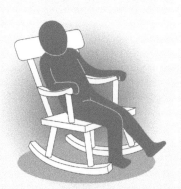

HOW THE *EGO STRUCTURE* INTERFERES WITH SPIRITUAL DIMENSION OF TYPE

Spiritual Dimension
Holy Love
Knowing that there is an underlying *love* and harmony in the world based on unconditional regard, respect and appreciation, combined with the state of being so present that you are fully awake and know exactly the *right action* to take

Psychological Ego Structure Interference
Trying to create harmony and respect among others and comfort in yourself by acquiescing to the desires of others, believing you don't matter enough to express yourself, and merging with others, forgetting yourself in the process

CHAPTER 2 | GETTING TYPE RIGHT

"Getting type right" is a phrase used among Enneagram teachers because accurate type identification is so important. But why? Why does it matter if a person identifies his or her Enneagram type accurately? Enneagram type is, after all, simply a number, one through nine.

"Getting type right" matters because your Enneagram type is not simply a number. Enneagram type is a precision point on a map revealing the interior landscape of the nine different human architectures. "Getting type right" especially matters if you want to use the Enneagram for personal growth, spiritual transformation or professional development. Accuracy in typing matters if an organization wants to use the Enneagram for leadership development or team effectiveness, culture change, decision-making, communication and more.

How do people get their type right? The answer to this can be extraordinarily simple or exceedingly complex. Here's a simple case of accurate typing.

A SIMPLE CASE OF TYPING

One night, I was on an airplane sitting next to a man in his mid-40s who asked me what I did professionally. When I mentioned the Enneagram, he became curious about what his type might be. I took the simple path with him, noting out loud that he seemed highly optimistic and asked if this were a correct observation. Hearing a convincing, strong yes from him, I suggested he might be one of the three optimistic types, 7, 9 or 2. When I described these three types, type 2 seemed to fit him perfectly.

SUMMARY: I asked the right questions and he was extremely self-aware, but it's often not this straightforward.

For many others, however, "getting type right" can be more challenging, especially when one or more of the following factors is present:

① Lack of self-awareness

② A complex background

③ An inexperienced Enneagram teacher

④ Focusing on behavior rather than motivation

⑤ Early trauma and other personal issues

⑥ Sole reliance on an Enneagram test

Whether a person is trying to type him- or herself by being in a workshop, using the results of an Enneagram test, reading Enneagram books, or conferring with an Enneagram teacher or coach, all of the above factors apply.

① Lack of self-awareness

To answer questions to find your type – from a teacher, a test, or reading a book – a person with low self-awareness cannot answer questions or describe him- or herself accurately. They will also tend to answer questions based on how they want to appear rather than how they actually are. And some people just don't know themselves very well.

TYPING ISSUE | LACK OF SELF-AWARENESS

Mike, a participant in an Enneagram training program, could not figure out his type at all, much less "get it right." Although he was sincere and interested, even after hearing verbal descriptions complete with graphics and examples and doing a typing card activity with guidance from the instructor, Mike couldn't eliminate any of the types. Mike was then asked, "Can you share three words that describe you well?" and he had no answer. Finally, Mike was asked, "Would you describe yourself as introspective or self-reflective?" and he had an answer: "No."

SUMMARY: It is very difficult for a low-aware person to determine his or her type without first spending time on self-awareness through self-observation and somatic sensing.

② A complex background

Some people have complex backgrounds for a variety of reasons. People can have cultural overlays on top of their real type. For example, Brazil has a very strong 7 culture and, as a result, many people from Brazil act a bit like 7s. For this reason, Brazilian 4s tend to be more positive than 4s from other countries; Brazilian 5s tend to talk a lot more and from an early age, though they do feel exhausted every day. Some people have a strong parental type-based overlay, and this can be from a parent or grandparent of any type. A dominant 6 parent, for example, can give many children in the family a tendency to doubt and be skeptical, even a 2 or 8 child. Understanding the complexity of a person's background can be useful when someone seems self-aware, yet can't quite find his or her type.

TYPING ISSUE | A COMPLEX BACKGROUND

Mary, a 40 year-old woman in a leadership program, was having problems identifying her type. She was very smart – she had been on the NASA alternate list for the Space Shuttle – and was very interested in her own development. Try as she did and with a great deal of guidance from the trainer, no clear type emerged. Mary dressed like a one-to-one subtype 4, wearing dramatic clothing that called attention to herself; related to other people like a 2, warmly asking many questions to create relationship; and she functioned in groups like a 9, being adept at tuning into a group and creating energetic harmony. Ultimately, the instructor gave Mary a copy of *The Wisdom of the Enneagram*, suggesting she read it and figure it out herself. Three months later, Mary realized she was a 1, but hadn't wanted to see this because her mother was a 1. She had wanted to be not-her-mother!

SUMMARY: It doesn't matter what you want to be; what is important is who you really are, but this can take time.

③ An inexperienced Enneagram teacher

Enneagram teachers and coaches do not intentionally mislead those who learn from them, yet this happens too often. Some teachers don't know what they don't know. They think they know when they don't. Enneagram teachers may have learned the Enneagram incorrectly from a teacher who wasn't experienced or knowledgeable enough to teach the Enneagram.

TYPING ISSUE | AN INEXPERIENCED ENNEAGRAM TEACHER

Just because someone has been exposed to the Enneagram doesn't mean they are ready to teach it. Here are some real quotes from teachers who have misled those under their guidance:

"All 6s have jutting jaws."

"You can't be a 4 because all 4s are unhappy."

"You can't be a 9 because you are not fat;
   9s eat their anger."

"You're innovative so you must be a 7."

"You intimidate me so you must be an 8."

"Only certain types are effective leaders;
   other types are not."

SUMMARY: These are cases of misinformation or teacher bias. Enneagram teachers need to be well-trained, well-informed and engage in their own personal work to reduce their own unintentional biases.

④ Focusing on behavior rather than motivation

Many people who first learn the Enneagram try to find their type through behaviors or qualities – for example, they ask questions such as *Which type has trouble saying no?* or *Which type is judgmental?* The problem with this line of inquiry is that several types have difficulty saying *no*, and almost all types can be judgmental. Different types simply have different reasons for engaging in similar behavior or manifesting similar qualities. What matters in accurately identifying type are the reasons underneath what we do or the qualities we possess – including motivations, mental habits and emotional patterns.

TYPING ISSUE | FOCUSING ON BEHAVIOR RATHER THAN MOTIVATION

Ann was a very smart woman who had been to every intensive Enneagram certification program available over a two-year period. However, she still did not know her type and became baffled when she went out into the organizational world to teach the Enneagram system to others. Highly frustrated, she did not know why she had such a challenge. The answer, however, was hiding in plain sight. Even with her extensive Enneagram training, Ann kept asking the wrong questions, such as *Which type works really hard?* or *Which type is sensitive?* The problem was this: "hard working" is a behavior; "sensitivity" is a quality. The Enneagram is Ego structure.

SUMMARY: While there are behaviors and qualities that correspond to each Enneagram type; these are not always unique to that type. As a result, you can't identify type on this basis.

⑤ Early trauma and other personal issues

Early trauma, whether a person has dealt effectively with these issues over time or not, often creates a unique complexity when identifying type. The reason for this is that a person with a great deal of early trauma may have had to engage in a variety of different coping strategies to deal with such extreme challenges. For example, they may have utilized their wings or arrow lines more than most other people. Traumatized individuals may also have big spaces of forgotten experiences and memories so they may not remember who they really are. However, the Enneagram can gently guide them in rediscovering themselves. It just takes longer to identify their type.

Other personal issues could include ADHD, Bipolar Disorder, Asperger's or some form of Autism, and Borderline Personality Disorder. A person with any of these can easily be mistyped. For example, individuals with ADHD can be mistyped as 7s due to their difficulty in staying focused. Someone who is bipolar, with mood swings going up and down, can be mistyped as a 4. People with Asperger's can get mistyped as 5s due to a tendency to display interpersonal awkwardness, although not all 5s are socially awkward. Borderline personalities can look like 4s because of their dramatic tendencies, but can also look like 6s because they tend to split others into good and bad.

TYPING ISSUE | EARLY TRAUMA AND OTHER PERSONAL ISSUES

James originally thought he was a counterphobic 6. Certainly, he was easily angered and would explode readily when provoked. And it didn't take much to provoke him. James was also aware that fear loomed large inside him, sometimes more frequently and sometime less so. James reasoned he was dealing with his fear by getting angry and fierce, just as this version of type 6 typically does. Counterphobic 6 also made a lot of sense because he would sometimes decompress by watching TV or playing video games, moving to type 9 (an arrow line of type 6) by spacing out.

All the above made sense until it didn't. After working on type 6 developmental issues and becoming even more aware, James realized that his early trauma played a role in this case of mistaken identity. His mother had a personality disorder; his father was violent. And James could never feel safe. Ultimately, James recognized that he was a 3, always wanting the recognition and approval from his parents that he could never seem to get. No matter how good his grades, how much he excelled in sports, nothing mattered. Yes, he used type 6 and type 9, but his essential nature was a 3. He was angry but not coming from a place of deep existencial anger, and he was fearful but not coming from existential fear. James was a 3, simply trying to be a "good boy" to gain acceptance that was beyond his family of origin's ability to provide.

SUMMARY: We never know a person's full background or how they responded to it. This can create layers upon layers over a type. But with patience and persistence, people will get there.

⑥ Sole reliance on an Enneagram test

Enneagram typing tests have added value to those of us teaching the Enneagram and who want to use them with clients. Individuals also avail themselves of typing tests on their own.

There are five commonly used tests – iEQ9, WEPSS, RHETI, Essential Enneagram, and EclecticEnergies. Most of these tests gives you a % score for which type or types you might be. For example, a test may indicate that there is an 85% chance you are a particular type and a 15% chance you are another type. Each test has been validated in its own way.

The problem occurs when people take the test and then assume the test has accurately identified their type, even if the test contains disclaimers. Even when test creators do not present the test results as definitive, test takers may take the results as if they are the absolute truth. This creates a problem for trainers and coaches who rely on tests rather than knowing the Enneagram well enough themselves to be able to help clients navigate whether or not the test results were accurate.

TYPING ISSUE | SOLE RELIANCE ON AN ENNEAGRAM TEST

In two different programs I led, one a Train-the-Trainer for a company and one for coaches online through a university, both groups had taken a typing test, although different tests. In both cases, only 60% of the participants had their types accurately identified. The good news was that they were open to exploring their real types, and this took some time. In other situations, however, individuals or groups often come to believe that the test results indicate their real types, even though this may be incorrect.

SUMMARY: If you find tests useful, that's fine. If you are an Enneagram teacher or coach, just make sure you know the Enneagram well yourself so you can guide others. If you are an individual trying to identify your type accurately, talk with an Enneagram professional and read at least two high-quality Enneagram books, in addition to considering the test results.

GETTING TYPE RIGHT WITH THE HELP OF DIFFERENTIATING QUESTIONS

Whether you use books, workshops, tests, interviews, or other approaches to determine Enneagram type, it is extremely common for people to ultimately narrow their choices to two types, but then not know where to go from there. For this reason, the next part of this book, Part II, offers three key questions you can ask that help people differentiate between each of the two types. Part II also includes (1) what to listen for when a person answers each question and (2) a graphical representation – a visual metaphor – of the two types doing the exact same activity but in two very different ways.

CHAPTER 3 | DIFFERENTIATING QUESTIONS

TYPE 1 VERSUS TYPE 2

The confusion between type 1 and type 2 does happen, most commonly because type 1 and type 2 are adjacent to one another on the Enneagram and, therefore, are wings of each other. A person might be a 1 with a 2 wing or a 2 with a 1 wing. In addition, because 1s tend to be polite and gracious, this behavior can be confused with the friendliness and helpfulness of most 2s.

QUESTION 1 | DETAIL-ORIENTATION
Do you focus on details? If so, when you focus on details, is this something you enjoy for its own sake, or do you do this in service of others?

Listen for this

Type 1 | If the person says, "for its own sake," this is more in the area of Enneagram 1s. Then ask them to share what they actually experience as they pursue details. Most 1s relish the details, enjoy the process of moving through things step by step, and find great satisfaction in putting order and structure into what might previously have been more chaotic or disorganized. As you listen to their answer, do they seem to take great satisfaction in putting things together in this way? If yes, then type 1 may be a good fit.

Type 2 | If the person says, "on behalf of others," ask them to share what about the service to others matters to them and if they would pursue details to such an extent if others were not impacted. As they talk, observe their level of genuine enthusiasm for others (as shown in their excitement or animation), as this is a good indication of type 2. While many 2s may be good at details (and some are not), most 2s don't love detail work unless it offers something of value to other people. Without the outside "customer" to consider, the amount of effort and time details take is not enough to keep 2s motivated.

QUESTION 2 | CENTERS OF INTELLIGENCE AND DECISION-MAKING
When you go about making important decisions or when you are discerning what you need to do about something that matters to you, what do you rely on most: Head, Heart, or Body?

Listen for this

Type 1 | Most 1s will be a little confused by this question, but will rarely say they use their Heart Center primarily. More often, they use their Head Center or Body Center or both. Although type 1 is formed in the Body (gut), some 1s think of themselves as more aligned with their minds than their guts. Many 1s experience an interplay between their minds and their guts, experiencing first a fast gut reaction, then their mind clicks in to explain their response.

Type 2 | Most 2s will readily say they rely on their Heart Center. Because they are an emotional center type, decisions must sit well with them emotionally, and important action almost always involves their values, feelings, and how they imagine others will respond.

QUESTION 3 | INTERNAL OR EXTERNAL FOCUS WHEN CALIBRATING ACTION

When you are calibrating what action to take, how to respond to something, and what choice you should make, is your calibration more on your internal processes and thoughts, or on how your action will be responded to by people in your external environment?

Listen for this

Type 1 | Although 1s and 2s will likely say both, there is usually a keen difference in (1) how much or what percentage is internal versus external, with 1s being more internal and 2s being more externally focused, and (2) the frequency of shuttling back and forth the person does as he or she goes about making the decision. 1s may shuttle between the internal and external, but only a small amount, with most of their time spent internally between their head and gut, then sometimes their heart.

Type 2 | 2s, by contrast, tend to focus more on the external than the internal and shuttle between the internal and external much more frequently and more rapidly. If the answer to the above question isn't clear, ask the person to give a recent example of how a decision was calibrated and listen for the internal versus external orientation.

- Hanging a picture -

TYPE 1 VERSUS TYPE 2

TYPE 1 VERSUS TYPE 3

The need for people to differentiate between types 1 and 3 is fairly common for several reasons. First, both types are part of the "competency triad," which means feeling competent and being perceived or treated as competent is very important to them (the third type that is part of this triad is type 5). Second, one of the subtypes of type 3 (the self-preserving subtype) is a look-alike for type 1, because self-preserving subtype 3s have more anxiety than the other two versions of 3 about getting whatever they are doing "right." Third, both 1s and 3s are planners, although they plan in different ways, with 1s constructing more detailed plans than 3s and also being more likely than 3s to have "to do" lists for almost everything.

QUESTION 1 | BEING RIGHT OR BEING EFFECTIVE
If you had to choose between being right and being effective, which would you choose and why?

Listen for this

Type 1 | Although 1s don't like this forced choice, their most ready response is, "Right." Then, listen to their explanation, which will be interesting in terms of the 1's vocabulary of "right," "wrong," "correct," "incorrect" and so forth. 1s like to be right (and dislike being wrong just as much if not more) and often think that being right is the same thing as being effective.

Type 3 | 3s also don't like this forced choice, but they might have to think about it longer than 1s. In the end, they will almost always choose effective. Jerry Wagner, in his book "Nine Lenses on the World," refers to 3s as "The Effective Person" because getting it right to them means getting something done effectively, a relative "right" rather than a more absolute "right," as would be more common among 1s.

QUESTION 2 | WHAT IS QUALITY?
As you think about how you define quality, which of these would better describe your definition: (1) quality means everything has to be done perfectly, even if the customer doesn't notice anything wrong, or (2) quality means that if the customer is satisfied and you add some extra value on top of their expectations, quality has been accomplished, even if the process and result are not exactly perfect?

Listen for this

Type 1 | Quality is defined solely according to the 1s' high standards, even if the customer doesn't perceive mistakes in what has been delivered. As a result, 1s will most often say the first definition aligns with their view of quality. For 1s, "good enough" or even "good enough plus" does not meet their standards of excellence. 1s will put in whatever time it takes to get all of it right because if they don't (and even if the customer doesn't notice), they will have lingering thoughts and feelings of self-recrimination that they didn't give it their all.

Type 3 | 3s define quality as meeting customer expectations and then adding extra value. However, to pursue tasks to perfection would be considered a waste of time and resources for most 3s. Even self-preservation subtype 3s, who are look-alikes for self-preservation subtype 1s, say they try to do as perfect a job as time allows. However, they move on when they run out of time, and something that was not done perfectly does not haunt them, particularly if the customer does not perceive any errors.

QUESTION 3 | RULES
You probably have a set of rules, principles and standards that are important to you. Is that true? If so, how many rules do you have, what categories of rules do these fall into (what areas), and can you give some examples?

Listen for this

Type 1 | 1s have so many rules, they can listed hundreds of them. In addition, their rules cover many areas and dimensions, from how to live your life, how to relate to others, how to organize your work, how to manage yourself and on and on.

Type 3 | 3s also have rules, but not nearly as many as 1s. In addition, 3s usually have them in more narrow areas – for example, work, planning, and many items that are role-based, since 3s often think in terms of roles such as parent, son or daughter, manager, worker, etc.

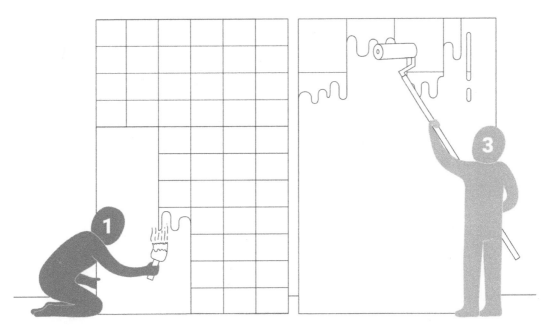

- Painting a wall -

© 2018 Ginger Lapid-Bogda PhD

TYPE 1 VERSUS TYPE 4

Some people may confuse Enneagram types 1 and 4, although this is not that common. These two types are, of course, arrow lines to one another, so there is usually some 4-ness in every type 1 and some 1-ness in type 4s, but the differences between the two types are more striking than the similarities.

The issues related to the confusion between these two types are (1) one of semantics (what is meant by certain word descriptors for each of these types, such as noticing "errors" for type 1 or noticing "what is missing" for type 4s); (2) whether a 1 is depressed quite frequently (in which case, they might believe themselves to be a 4); or (3) whether the "inner critic" of the 4 is extremely active (in which case, the 4 might mistake him- or herself to be a 1).

QUESTION 1 | AESTHETIC PREFERENCES

When you think about your aesthetic preferences, do you prefer something precise and detailed in which there are no flaws whatsoever, or do you have a more symbolic, expressive aesthetic where the precise details matter far less than the personal and universal nature of the work?

Listen for this

Type 1 | 1s prefer a precise, detailed, and flawless artistic expression, whether the aesthetic be one of their own making or something created by someone else. They notice a musical note that is flat, a line of poetry that is wordy or trite, a novel that uses incorrect grammar or punctuation, words that are used incorrectly and more. Simply put, their eyes, ears and sensibilities are wired to notice these things as mistakes, and this irritates 1s.

Type 4 | 4s have an aesthetic that is more symbolic and expressive, where precise details are less significant than the overall impact and beauty of the art, whether self or other created. At times, too much detail, at least in the eyes of the 4, can actually detract from the significance or impact of the art. Said another way, 4s are not seeking flawlessness; they are trying to express meaning. This distinction can be a bit confusing because 4s will notice something that is missing aesthetically, but this may not be a literal mistake.

QUESTION 2 | STRUCTURE AND RULES

As you think about how you interact with others and your environment, would you describe yourself as a structured person who likes to have things organized (mostly by you), with clear and distinct rules for people's behavior and roles? Or, would you describe yourself as a more fluid person, who likes more of a minimalist structure and a few rules because you think that too much structure and too many rules constrict both you and the creative process?

Listen for this

Type 1 | 1s like clear rules and quite a lot of structure because when these are present, they then know what to do and how to do it. Even more important, fewer errors will occur (or so they think). Interestingly, many 1s enjoy a bit of disorder initialy because they can then figure out a better structure and a clear set of rules, roles, and responsibilities.

Type 4 | From the 4 perspective, too many rules and roles and too much structure will limit the creative possibilities and their own freedom of expression, both of which matter to them a great deal. For 4s, self-expression, creativity, and the generation of something new and original requires flexibility and emergent structure, just enough to enable them to manifest what they desire without constraining their originality.

QUESTION 3 | GUT AND HEAD OR HEART IN DECISION-MAKING
What is your process for making most decisions in your life? Do you make them from your gut and your head together (more specifically, your gut reacts and then your head gives words and meaning to your instinctual decision)? Or, do you make decisions from your heart, including feeling responses from both you and others?

Listen for this

Type 1 | 1s may think they reach decisions from their minds, but more aware 1s realize it starts in the body (in their gut) and then their minds give reasons that explain the rationale for their gut's responses. But whether they think their reactions start in the gut or the mind, 1s rarely say their responses start in the Heart Center.

Type 4 | For 4s, the heart rules their world because they identify so strongly with being a "feeling" person. Although some 4s (primarily those 4s with a 5 wing) might say their minds are very active in decision-making or in helping construct their responses, rarely will 4s say their responses are from their gut (Body Center).

- Painting a vase -

TYPE 1 VERSUS TYPE 4

Sometimes people do get confused as to whether they are type 1 or type 5, and this lack of clarity does make sense. Both 1s and 5s are part of the "competency triad" (along with type 3), meaning of all the nine types, 1s, 3s and 5s care most about feeling competent themselves and being perceived as competent by others. 3s are the most readily distinguishable of this triad because competence in their minds is defined as getting results. For 1s, competence is about being right, whereas for 5s, competence means knowledge-based competence. One way to understand the distinction between competence for type 1 versus type 5 is that "being right" for 1s has to be with just about everything from the way they think to how they plan and execute, as well as their opinions. For 5s, competence is what they know, which they do not regard as opinions but view as facts.

QUESTION 1 | TIME, ENERGY AND BOUNDARIES

Are you willing – and even think it is your responsibility – to consistently work extra hours if necessary to get something right, or do you strongly prefer to set and keep exact boundaries on the amount of time you are willing to spend on something?

Listen for this

Type 1 | 1s, even when tired, are more than willing – even if they feel resentful about this over time – to spend numerous extra hours on projects or tasks to make sure all the information is correct, that it is executed properly, and that there are no mistakes of any kind. In other words, they go over the details completely and feel personally responsible for delivering a product that is as close to perfect as possible.

Type 5 | 5s are strong boundary setters because their energy becomes extremely depleted with too much work, too much interaction with others, plus a number of other factors. They know that if they extend past their allotted time or pre-set boundaries, they will feel utterly drained of vitality and energy. So while 5s like things to be done well, they neither have the reserves to consistently put in these extraordinary hours nor the sense of responsibility that they must always do so (on occasion, yes, they will; as a matter of normal working, no).

QUESTION 2 | SELF-CONTROL OR SELF-CONTAINMENT

Do you experience yourself as exerting self-control so that you try to not show or express anger or displeasure to others – although others can often "read" you well through your body language – and try to keep yourself on the path to appropriate behavior? Or, are you self-contained where you keep your energy and responses more within yourself so that most people find you "hard to read?"

Listen for this

Type 1 | 1s believe that "good" and polite people don't show anger directly, although 1s do relate to feeling frustrated or upset, yet try to control its outward expression. However, in most cases, others find 1s fairly easy to read, as their displeasure often appears through body language (grimaces and frowns) and through their voice tone. In terms of other emotions such as joy, sadness and anxiety, 1s are reasonably transparent as they may express these emotions verbally or show them through non-verbal cues, even to people who don't know them well.

Type 5 | 5s are masters of self-containment, with low-level animation in their voices and non-verbal behavior. This, combined with their consistent and automatic disconnection from feelings, makes them challenging for most people to read based on their external cues.

QUESTION 3 | DOING OR THINKING
When approaching a situation that potentially requires action, do you get an immediate gut sense of what to do, then use your mind to establish the plan and move quickly to action, or do you rely on your mind to understand and analyze the situation and take the time you believe you need to determine what action to take?

Listen for this

Type 1 | 1s usually have an immediate gut reaction in terms of what to do (believing this is likely the right way to proceed), analyze quickly to create the related rationale, and then move to action quite quickly, enjoying the ability to fix something or solve the problem. In this sense, action originates from their Body Center.

Type 5 | 5s, in general, don't move to quick action – far more slowly when compared to 1s – as 5s usually want to collect and analyze all the relevant information before they determine what action to take. In this sense, action stems from their Head Center.

- Fixing a car -

TYPE 1 VERSUS TYPE 5

The confusion between type 1 and type 6 happens fairly often. The issue is primarily related to the subtypes, and in particular, the self-preservation subtype 1 – called "worry"– can be confused with type 6, primarily the self-preservation subtype 6, called "warmth." Also confusing at times is the social subtype 6 – called "duty" – and the social subtype 1, called "non-adaptability."

Self-preservation subtype 1s worry about getting it right, being as close to perfect as possible themselves, and need to have everything under control. But they worry before something occurs, and once they understand how to get it right, the worry stops. 6s who palpably worry usually do so before, during, and after something occurs. Their worry isn't so much about getting it right as it is to keep something bad from happening as a result of something going wrong.

Social subtype 6s dearly want to know what the external rules are, and they adhere to them so they don't get in trouble. Social subtype 1s already know what the rules are – their rules are internalized already – so there is no need to seek them from the outside.

QUESTION 1 | PLANNING
When you plan, does your planning come from your gut or from your mind?

Listen for this

Type 1 | 1s almost always say from their gut first and then their mind puts words to their gut-sense of the right plan. Occasionally, 1s may say their minds, but if you ask further probing questions about where the planning actually starts, 1s will say their guts. In addition, the way in which 1s plan is neither simple nor complex, although it is often thorough.

Type 6 | 6s plan from their minds, almost always. In fact, their minds come up with multiple pathways to get from A to B. The more complex the challenge, the more their minds get stimulated, and the mental planning of 6s is rarely simple and is often highly complex.

QUESTION 2 | CONSEQUENCES OF NOT GETTING IT RIGHT
When approaching a decision or an action, do you become concerned about not doing it right, not doing it perfectly and making a mistake, or are you more focused on all the negative things that might happen, particularly from external forces, as a result of not doing it right?

Listen for this

Type 1 | 1s want to get it right because it's the right thing to do for its own sake, not primarily because something negative or bad will occur if they don't. When 1s don't get it right, they engage in self-recrimination or become defensive and blame others. So ask them about how they react when a mistake does occur. If it's self-recrimination (anger directed at self) or blame (anger directed at others), the person is more likely a 1.

Type 6 | 6s want to get things right because they don't want to get in trouble from outside sources – for example, authority figures, peers, family. They can also get in trouble with themselves, beating themselves up mentally and emotionally, but their initial focus of concern is more often external than internal. 6s are not really perfectionists, needing everything to be perfect and go perfectly. They just don't want to do something wrong that might cause harm to themselves or others.

QUESTION 3 | A RIGHT WAY
Do you think that, in most cases, there is a right way to do just about anything, or do you believe that there are almost always multiple ways to proceed forward, each of which has positive aspects and downsides?

Listen for this

Type 1 | 1s, if they are honest and they usually are, will say there usually is one right way to approach something. If the 1 is not as aware or wants to give what they believe is the correct answer (i.e., that there is more than one right way), he or she might say there can be multiple right ways. What is important to listen to is the belief that there is a right way – not to be confused with a best way – to do just about anything.

Type 6 | 6s don't really believe there is a singular right way to do anything. Instead, they believe in contingencies, and generate alternative paths to approach a situation. Their thinking is similar to a risk assessment analysis – for example, 6s will think, if we do this, that will happen but if we do that, this will happen. They project outcomes into the future and select from among them.

- Playing football -

© 2018 Ginger Lapid-Bogda PhD

TYPE 1 VERSUS TYPE 6

TYPE 1 VERSUS TYPE 7

The confusion between type 1 and type 7 is not common because they are so very different. 1s are the most self-controlled of all nine Enneagram types, and 7s are the most spontaneous or impulsive. 1s are a Body Center type, while 7s clearly reside in the Head Center, with all their elaborate and fast moving idea generation. 1s are pragmatic realists, and 7s are the eternal optimists. However, some people do get confused, primarily because these two types are on an arrow line to one another. As a result, 7s may utilize some qualities of type 1, and 1s may relate to some qualities of type 7.

QUESTION 1 | HOW YOUR MIND WORKS

Do you have a linear, logical and structured mind, or do you have a mind that continuously and quickly comes up with explosions of new ideas and thoughts, so that the ideas are connected to one another but not in a structured, organized way?

Listen for this

Type 1 | 1s have extraordinarily structured, logical, organized minds, akin to linear lists or structured outlines. That's just how they think!

Type 7 | 7s have minds like computer desktops on which there are no folders, only desktop files with connections between them. Their minds are not linear, but neither are they circular. Their minds are more like continuous and rapid brainstorms or loosely organized mind maps.

QUESTION 2 | CONTROL OR IMPULSIVITY

Would you describe yourself as a self-controlled and highly structured person, or are you more free-wheeling, fluid, spontaneous and even impulsive?

Listen for this

Type 1 | 1s are extremely self-controlled, keeping themselves in check so they don't make mistakes or get something wrong, and they do this to feel in control of themselves and their immediate environment. Otherwise, 1s can become anxious when they experience a lack of things being in their proper place.

Type 7 | 7s are the opposite of 1s with respect to control. They like and demand maximum freedom, and as a result, they do not like structure very much as they believe structure is constraining and limiting. They like to think of themselves as continuously spontaneous and some will admit to being impulsive, although they prefer to label this as freedom and spontaneity.

QUESTION 3 | DETAIL AND TIMELINESS
Are you good at and really like dealing with details, plus insist on being on time for almost everything you do, or do you engage in details only when you have to in order to get the job done and timeliness is not your strength?

Listen for this

Type 1 | 1s like detail so much, they often focus on detail throughout a project or task. Details have an importance to 1s in terms of the quality of the final product, and they often think, "The devil is in the details." They also just enjoy rolling up their sleeves and doing detailed work, often being reluctant to give this over to others. In terms of timeliness, 1s are the most "on-time" of all the types, although they might occasionally be late for a meeting, a deliverable or even a lunch appointment.

Type 7 | 7s are not big fans of details; they are more interested in the ideas and the stimulation of a new project than the attention to detail all along the way. Sometimes, 7s will say they are good at detail, but what they really mean is that they will pay close attention near the end of a project (this would be perceived to others as last minute), swooping in with perfectionistic fervor to try to make sure it is a job well done. In terms of time, 7s think they can control time so that linear time doesn't really apply to them. Consequently, they may be late to meetings, late delivering a product, or late for lunch. Sometimes, they apologize for this; other times, they may say nothing or reframe why they were late, putting a positive spin on their behavior.

- Enjoying a gourmet meal -

TYPE 1 VERSUS TYPE 7

TYPE 1 VERSUS TYPE 8

The confusion between type 1 and type 8 happens occasionally, primarily because both 1s and 8s are Body Center types and so share a special, although different, relationship to anger and control. In addition, one-to-one subtype 1s, called "zeal," can be very forward and intense, seemingly like 8s.

QUESTION 1 | MICRO OR MACRO-MANAGING

When you manage or oversee a project, do you normally micro-manage the activities from start to end and enjoy this, or do you prefer to macro-manage the big picture and end results, preferring to leave the day-to-day details to others?

Listen for this

Type 1 | 1s love details and like to micro-manage activities, including their own efforts and those of others. In addition to enjoying checking up and holding people accountable in order to get things right, 1s also believe that if they don't do this, mistakes are inevitable and could have been easily avoided. And all of that, 1s believe, is their responsibility.

Type 8 | 8s really like to macro-manage big projects and large challenges and don't like detail, even if some 8s are good at it (and most are not very good at it). As a result, 8s do not like to micro-manage and only do so when they don't trust the other person to do the job effectively or when the 8 feels under a great deal of pressure and believes he or she shouldn't share this burden with others.

QUESTION 2 | HOW DO YOU EXPRESS YOUR ANGER?

How do you most commonly relate to and express your anger? Do you view the expression of robust anger as something you think self-controlled and polite people should refrain from doing and relate more to irritation, frustration, and being resentful or upset? Or, do you perceive anger as simply energy that needs to be expressed and released soon after it occurs?

Listen for this

Type 1 | 1s believe that expressing anger directly is impolite, and they typically have enough self-control not to do so. In fact, most 1s don't like the word anger, preferring to describe that emotion as distress, upset, resentment or irritation. Still, anger is the emotional fuel that drives the type, even if they thwart its complete expression.

Type 8 | 8s directly express their anger in most cases, and their anger can be big and energetic. They perceive this as honesty, plus the direct immediate expression of feeling allows them to not store it or somatize it in their bodies. Unlike 1s, 8s rarely feel guilty for feeling and sharing their anger. The exception to this is if they unintentionally hurt someone else they care for. There are some 8s who don't express anger so readily, but this is usually the result of some early childhood or early adult experiences that they experienced as traumatic in some way.

QUESTION 3 | HOW DO YOU EXERT CONTROL?

Is your way of controlling situations to be very self-controlled and to try to control your immediate environment, or do you try to control the whole, big picture more than yourself or the specific circumstances?

Listen for this

Type 1 | 1s exert control by being highly self-controlled and by trying to control the details of their specific environment. Doing so reduces their anxiety about not doing it right or making a mistake.

Type 8 | 8s do not customarily exhibit much self-control; they are more apt to go after exactly what they want when they want it. They don't pay the same kind of attention as 1s to being polite or behaving in a socially proper way. In addition, they rarely concern themselves, unless highly stressed, with controlling the specifics of a situation and are far more likely to think big picture. If they don't control the larger enviroment, 8s believe that everything may fall apart in front of them.

- Working out -

TYPE 1 VERSUS TYPE 8

The confusion between type 1 and type 9 does happen, most likely because type 1 and type 9 are adjacent to one another on the Enneagram and, therefore, are wings of each other. A person might be a 1 with a 9 wing or a 9 with a 1 wing. In addition, both 1s and 9s can be stubborn, although in two different ways. For example, 1s can be firm and stubborn about their way being the right way, whereas 9s become highly stubborn when they perceive someone else telling them what to do. Even suggesting a course of action that a 9 doesn't want to take can activate the "Don't try to control me" response in 9s; however, 9s rarely say this out loud. Instead, they are more likely to appear compliant, but have no intention of following through on what was suggested.

QUESTION 1 | HAVING AND STATING YOUR OPINIONS
Do you have many strong opinions and express them both verbally and nonverbally, or do you more often keep your opinions to yourself and don't express them so as to not create tension or conflict?

Listen for this

Type 1 | 1s have many, many opinions and they express them quite often, even though they may keep some to themselves. However, even when they don't share their opinions verbally, their body language often indicates whether or not they like or dislike something or whether they agree or disagree with an idea. Most 1s are very easy to read.

Type 9 | 9s tend to not express their opinions, even if it's a question of where they prefer to go to dinner. With larger and more important items, they are even more reluctant to share so as to not generate tension or distress.

QUESTION 2 | EXPRESSING JUDGMENTS OR APPEARING HIGHLY TOLERANT
Do you see yourself – and even more importantly, do other people see you – as a person who is judging and discerns easily, or as a person who is tolerant, non-judging and more easy-going and accepting?

Listen for this

Type 1 | 1s judge almost everything: food, people, plays, music, events, and more. It is obvious when 1s like or dislike something and whether they agree with something or do not. They live in a world where things are right or wrong and correct or incorrect.

Type 9 | 9s are the most easy-going type of all nine Enneagram types. Although they may have judgments about certain things, they have dramatically fewer judgments than do 1s. 9s are also the most accepting and tolerant of all the nine types, a quality that makes others feel they can talk to 9s about issues without being judged or criticized.

QUESTION 3 | BEING DIRECT OR INDIRECT
Would you call yourself a direct person, or do you think of yourself as more indirect and diplomatic?

Listen for this

Type 1 | 1s are among the most direct of the Enneagram types. 1s also value honesty, and they also have quick reaction times, which contributes to their being straightforward. Although 1s are polite, they are usually polite in a clear and direct way.

Type 9 | 9s, by contrast are usually indirect; the only type similarly indirect are 2s, yet some 2s can be quite direct. The 9s' indirectness comes from a variety of sources: wanting to explain context before getting to their point; needing to tell a whole story sequentially, then believing that the message is obvious in the whole story and doesn't need to be said directly; and sometimes not being quite sure of their exact point until they explore it out loud.

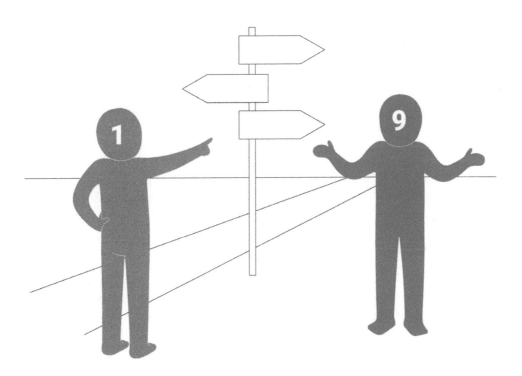

- Stating their opinions -

© 2018 Ginger Lapid-Bogda PhD

The confusion between type 2 and type 3 is quite common, primarily because both 2s and 3s are Heart Center types who are attuned to the reactions of others. They also sit adjacent on the Enneagram symbol and, therefore, are wings of one another. A person might be a 2 with a 3 wing or a 3 with a 2 wing.

In addition, there can be an interesting combination of sweetness and toughness in both 2s and 3s. On the outside, 2s appear sweeter and kinder; however, many 2s have a strong inner will or backbone made of stainless steel. 3s, by contrast, can appear a little tougher on the outside, as if nothing really bothers them, but inside, many 3s are tender, sensitive, and kind.

QUESTION 1 | BEING LIKED OR BEING RESPECTED
What is more important to you, being liked by others or being respected by them?

Listen for this

Type 2 | 2s will almost always say being liked, and there is rarely a pause when they say this. One way 2s get others to like them is by being helpful and attentive. On occasion, older 2s may say something like they have spent a lot of time and energy over the years to be liked, and now, they would prefer to be respected. This response still fits the type 2 profile.

Type 3 | 3s will almost always say respect. In fact, many 3s don't care so much whether others like them unless they have the belief that others won't give respect unless they also like someone. In other words, being liked is a prerequisite to being respected. Some 3s will have to think about this question a while – that is, they may not give a fast answer – but they end up choosing respect.

QUESTION 2 | PURPOSE OR GOALS
Do you live and work more from intention and purpose, or do you live and work from pursuing specific goals and developing efficient plans to accomplish them?

Listen for this

Type 2 | 2s do not work from specific, concrete goals and plans, at least not that often. More frequently, 2s work from a heartfelt sense of intention or purpose. Specific goals, in general, do not help most 2s accomplish what they want to do. It is possible some 2s may say they have goals, so ask what they mean by goals; their definition is rarely specific, measurable, etc.

Type 3 | 3s are almost always focused on specific goals and plans. In fact, without specific goals, 3s become anxious and even disoriented. Goals and plans help them (1) feel competent to accomplish what they set out to do and (2) provide them with a sense of structure for their actions.

QUESTION 3 | EMOTIONAL PATIENCE OR IMPATIENCE
When exploring emotions, either by yourself or with others, would you describe yourself as patient or impatient?

Listen for this

Type 2 | 2s are usually quite patient when listening to other people's emotions unless the other person is constantly complaining and doing nothing about it. Other than this, 2s like to be available to others and are generous with their time. Even if someone is angry with the 2 – which 2s don't like very much – 2s will listen to the other person. And when 2s themselves are feeling emotional and ready to express it, they want the other person to spend time listening in return.

Type 3 | 3s become quickly impatient with emotional conversations, even if they find some value in them initially (which sometimes they do and sometimes not). But if the conversation goes on at any length, if the topic of conversation is one the 3 would rather avoid, and/or if the 3 has some work to do, 3s will try to cut off the conversation early. Unless the 3 has done a great deal of work in the emotional arena, 3s are not usually comfortable experiencing or expressing their own feelings, especially sorrow and anxiety.

- Running a marathon -

TYPE 2 VERSUS TYPE 3

TYPE 2 VERSUS TYPE 4

The confusion between type 2 and type 4 occurs frequently, primarily because (1) both 2s and 4s are Heart Center types, sharing the common emotion of sadness or sorrow as an underlying emotional state and creating an image as a substitute for who they are underneath the image; (2) both are emotional types who are attuned to feelings, although 2s attune to the feelings of others and 4s attune more to their own feelings; and (3) both sit on the Enneagram symbol as arrow lines of one another. A person might be a 2 with strong access to his or her 4 arrow or a 4 with strong access to his or her 2 arrow.

There is another reason for possible confusion between these two Enneagram types. Enneagram 2s and 4s are akin to cousins where they share a similar sense of the world: *The world is full of joy and suffering.* Based on this shared felt-sense, 2s take the path of *I must help alleviate the suffering of others*, and 4s take the path of *I must first go into my own suffering to get to the personal and universal experience of joy.* When attempting to discern whether type 2 or type 4 is a better fit, some people struggle because in many 2s, there can be a great deal of type 4 and vice versa.

QUESTION 1 | JOY AND SUFFERING
In a world filled with joy and suffering, do you think it is your job to help keep others from suffering, or is it to go into your own suffering to then find the joy?

Listen for this

Type 2 | 2s will almost always say that their role or job is to help others to not suffer if possible. They will then often describe how they do this, especially if probed to provide clarification. Listen for these kinds of statements: listening to others, providing advice, offering resources, and simply being compassionate.

Type 4 | 4s will almost always have to ponder this question, partly because 4s ponder most things to make sure the answer they give is what they truly think; 2s rarely have to ponder this specific question. Upon reflection, 4s will say that they do have to understand themselves before they can offer understanding to others, and this requires going into their own suffering before they can find their own joy.

QUESTION 2 | PEOPLE LIKING YOU
Do you tend to assume that most people are going to like you and are surprised and then confused when they don't? Or, do you come from a perspective of not being sure if people will like you and (1) accept this as the way life is for you and (2) become concerned about what might not be good-enough about you?

Listen for this

Type 2 | 2s will indicate they are used to people liking them and may even be honest enough to admit that they believe they can get almost anyone they want to like them if they put their attention to this. Don't mistake this for 2s saying they want everyone to like them, just that they think most people do.

Type 4 | 4s are far more attuned to feeling deficient or not-good-enough rather than coming from the assumption that people, in general, will like them. If the question is phrased *Is it important that people like you*, 2s and 4s will both say *yes*, so make sure to ask about the assumptions of likeability rather than the importance of it.

> ### QUESTION 3 | FEELINGS
> With respect to emotions, do you tend to focus first on other people's feelings more than your own, or does your attention first go to experiencing and exploring your own feelings?

Listen for this

Type 2 | 2s, unless they are really upset, focus more on the feelings of others first. In addition, 2s repress their feelings, not knowing exactly what they feel in the moment or how deeply they feel something. They generally know they are experiencing some form of emotion, but not always the nature and depth of the feeling.

Type 4 | 4s almost always go inward first to examine their own emotional reactions, which are usually quite intense. Most 4s believe the statement *I am my feelings*, so they not only value their own feelings, their feelings are often so strong or complicated that they feel compelled to explore them.

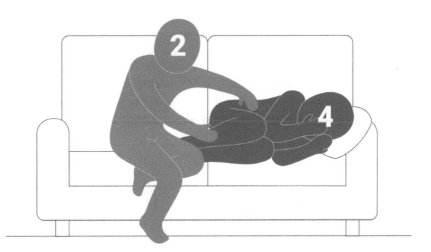

- Dealing with sorrow -

TYPE 2 VERSUS TYPE 4

The confusion between type 2 and type 5 is not really that common for a number of reasons. First, 2s are formed in the Heart Center and are typically very warm and not hesitant to ask about the feelings of others. In fact, 2s ask others many questions of all kinds, with 2s perceiving this as a way of establishing and maintaining a good relationship.

5s, by contrast, are an Enneagram type formed in the Head Center, and they deal with the Head Center's central emotion of fear by cutting off from their feelings in real time, but also by withdrawing or pulling away from direct engagement with others. 5s rarely share their emotions with others unless they really trust the person and are the least likely of all Enneagram types to ask inquisitive questions about another person's feeling state or personal life. Unless the 5 is a therapist or a coach, most 5s consider these types of questions to be intrusive and an invasion of the other person's privacy. In addition, 5s generally don't like to discuss emotions for very long (if at all) unless they are with a significant other whom they deeply trust, and even then, 5s get drained easily by such conversations if these go on very long.

QUESTION 1 | ABUNDANCE OR SCARCITY
Do you believe that the world is filled with an abundance of resources that should be shared with others, or is the world comprised of scarce resources that need to be conserved?

Listen for this

Type 2 | 2s believe in abundance – sometimes "false abundance," although they think it is real – so they are willing to give almost all of it away because, in their minds, there is always more. This includes food, time, energy, money and more. If you think the person is a 2, ask them for examples of this giving from abundance.

Type 5 | 5s will often cringe when they think about giving away their resources, primarily because they perceive these as scarce. Why would you give them away and be depleted! So watch for the cringe or the retracted body language right after you ask the question, and also listen to determine if the person's comments are consistent with the scarcity model or paradigm. In contrast to 2s, it can be said that 5s live in a world of "false scarcity."

QUESTION 2 | EMPATHY
When someone is experiencing an emotional difficulty and you are in this person's presence, do you experience the other person's feelings internally, almost as if they were your own, or do you listen with concern but are more detached from your own emotional reaction?

Listen for this

Type 2 | 2s are among the most empathic of the nine Enneagram types, often experiencing another's feelings somatically before the other person has expressed what is occurring. In a way, 2s can be empathic sponges, particularly when the other person's feelings are deep and compelling, but even when they are not.

Type 5 | 5s detach emotionally in real time most of the time unless they have done a great deal of self-development work to learn how to experience and integrate their feelings in real time. Most 5s will be aware enough to know they disconnect emotionally when another person's feelings are intense, noting that intense feelings feel overwhelming.

QUESTION 3 | EMOTIONS OR LOGIC
Which do you trust more, emotions or logic, and which do you distrust more, emotions or logic?

Listen for this

Type 2 | 2s, as a Heart Center type, trust feeling more than logic. 2s perceive a reliance on logic as either too mental or they view an over-adherence to logic as a means to justify or rationalize something. 2s would say there are actually many forms of logic, all of which can be used to justify just about anything. It's not that 2s always trust feelings and never logic; it's that when given the choice, most 2s will select emotions.

Type 5 | 5s believe the opposite. They believe that logic can and should be trusted because logic is objective, whereas emotions are subjective, volatile and, therefore, inherently untrustworthy.

- Going to a birthday party -

© 2018 Ginger Lapid-Bogda PhD

TYPE 2 VERSUS TYPE 5

The confusion between type 2 and type 6 is not really that common, but it can happen if the person is a self-preservation subtype of either type. Self-preservation subtype 6s are called "warm" 6s, and they use their warmth and friendliness as a hedge against their anxieties and insecurities. They draw people to them with their warmth and forge strong bonds, unconsciously reasoning that there is safety in the protection of the group. Self-preservation subtype 2s are the most anxious of the 2s, and they can appear to need and want the protection of others. These 2s are also less trusting and more worried than the other two subtypes of 2 and, thus, share some similarities with self-preservation subtype 6s.

QUESTION 1 | WHY YOU DO THINGS FOR OTHERS
When you do things for others, is your concern more about others liking you and being needed by them, or more about loyalty and feeling safe and secure?

Listen for this

Type 2 | 2s will say being liked and needed with very little to say about safety. Most 2s will also tell you they like doing things for others, at least most of the time. Their self-image of being a generous person gets reinforced when they do things for others that are then valued or appreciated.

Type 6 | 6s may have to think about this far more than 2s – so pay attention to the amount of "thought time" involved – but they will almost always say being loyal and secure or safe is what really drives their behavior.

QUESTION 2 | WORRY
Would you describe yourself as someone who worries a lot, and if you do, what do you tend to worry about?

Listen for this

Type 2 | 2s generally say they don't worry about that much or if they do say yes, then ask him or her about the kinds of things that are concerns. Listen closely because if they have someone close to them who is dying or if money is scarce right now, anyone of any type would likely be worried. 2s may say they worry about people and relationships, but not much else. As a note, self-preservation subtype 2s worry more than the other two subtypes of type 2, but not as much as 6s.

Type 6 | 6s will rattle off a long list of what they worry about, and the areas they worry about are endless, not just about people and relationships. Self-preserving subtype 6s tend to worry the most because they use worry and doubt as a way to consider everything possible and plan against those things occurring. Social subtype 6s also worry or anticipate with regularity. One-to-one subtype 6s may not relate to worry, but ask them if they do a lot of instantaneous problem solving.

QUESTION 3 | RISK
How do you relate to risk in your life?

Listen for this

Type 2 | 2s either have to think a lot about this question to arrive at an answer – which means they don't really think about risk all that much; otherwise they would have a ready answer – or they will simply ask you what you mean by risk. This lack of a clear and immediate answer tells you most of what you need to know. Risk is not that central to them or their way of thinking.

Type 6 | 6s are the opposite of 2s when discussing risk. 6s will have a lot to say about this topic: they like it or they don't like it. They like it sometimes but not at other times. They are deathly afraid of risk, and it also excites them. Just listen for an abundance of strong feelings and many thoughts about risk that go in many different directions.

- Staying warm by the campfire -

TYPE 2 VERSUS TYPE 6

TYPE 2 VERSUS TYPE 7

The confusion between type 2 and type 7 is reasonably common, even though there are distinct differences between the two types. 2s and 7s form part of what is called the "optimistic triad," which means they (along with type 9) tend to have a positive outlook on life, even embellishing reality. Amplifying this confusion, social subtype 7, called "sacrifice," is a look-alike for type 2. These 7s will sacrifice their need to have what they want when they want it on behalf of the group – at least, momentarily – and may appear to themselves to be more like 2s.

QUESTION 1 | FEELINGS
How do you know what someone else is feeling, through your heart or through your mind?

Listen for this

Type 2 | 2s know immediately what another feels because they read the feelings of others through their heart. Sometimes 2s will say doing this is so intuitive, they are not even sure exactly where this comes from or how they do this. Some 2s will say they feel or experience the feelings of others by merely being in the other person's presence.

Type 7 | 7s may have to think about this far more than 2s, so pay attention to both the amount of "thought time" and the clarity of response. 7s may either be confused by this question, say their "heart" but in an unconvincing manner almost as if this is speculative. They may say this: "I read people with my mind," or "I'm not very good at reading other people."

QUESTION 2 | APPRECIATION
If you do something generous for others, what do you want in return, implicit appreciation from the other person or an explicit and even public thank-you for your sacrifice?

Listen for this

Type 2 | 2s generally say that what they offered was simply a generous act with nothing expected in return. In reality, 2s want appreciation and a sense of being valued for what they do for others; however, many 2s are not aware that their giving is not as selfless as they want to believe. That said, most 2s do not need or want public appreciation – it can be embarrassing – and they do not usually perceive their giving to others as a sacrifice.

Type 7 | 7s, specifically social subtype 7s (called "sacrifice"), want to be acknowledged explicitly for the sacrifice of not giving into their gluttony or desire to have what they want immediately. Claudio Naranjo, the leading expert on Enneagram subtypes, tells this story about social subtype 7s: "A 7 went to the ice cream store with her friends. As an act of sacrifice, the 7 let all of her friends get their ice cream first, then went behind the counter and got two scoops of ice cream, not just one. In addition, she stood in front of her friends, basking in their acknowledgment of her sacrifice on their behalf."

QUESTION 3 | FOCUS

Would you describe yourself as a person for whom focusing on one thing for an extended time is not particularly challenging, or as someone who must exert a concerted effort to focus because you get easily distracted by external stimuli?

Listen for this

Type 2 | Most 2s can focus pretty easily most of the time for short, medium and long periods of time. The exception to this is when they are extremely excited or depressed, angry or anxious. However, most of the time, 2s are even-tempered, so focusing is not a particular challenge. They may get distracted at times, but easily return to the project or task at hand.

Type 7 | 7s are the opposite of 2s; focusing is not only difficult, it can be painful and highly stressful. Because the 7's mind is constantly and rapidly moving, focusing on one thing feels challenging and restrictive. In addition, the lack of focus enables 7s to easily shift their attention to external stimuli; this keeps them stimulated, excited, and more able to run away from distress or unpleasantness.

- Reading a book -

TYPE 2 VERSUS TYPE 7

TYPE 2 VERSUS TYPE 8

The confusion between type 2 and type 8 is reasonably common, especially, but not only, among women. The reason for this is that 2s and 8s are on arrow lines of one another; some 8 women, depending on their culture and family context, may perceive type 8 as too bold or "masculine" and gravitate to their 2 arrow line.

Male and female 2s also access their 8 arrow line when they get angry, access their own power, and take a strong stand on issues. Thus, 2s can, at times, be a force to be reckoned with, much like 8s. Similarly, when 8s are comfortable and open-hearted, they can be generous and deeply compassionate, much like 2s.

In addition, social subtype 2s and social subtype 8s can be confused for several reasons: (1) both focus on leading and taking care of groups; (2) both are more intellectual than the other subtypes of their type; and (3) social subtype 2s are more likely to "own their own power" than the other two subtypes of 2 and can, therefore, look more like 8s.

QUESTION 1 | LEADERSHIP
Do you believe you were born to support others and will lead others only when it is necessary, or were you born to lead, organize and make big things happen?

Listen for this

Type 2 | 2s will step into leadership, especially social subtype 2s, but they don't seek it out, nor do they feel compelled or born to lead. Supporting others is more on their minds and in their hearts, and as a result, most 2s will say born to support rather than born to lead.

Type 8 | 8s feel they were born to lead, with an instinctive ability and desire to get things under control and move people and activities forward. Although some 8s don't support others very much and others do quite a bit, the support 8s offer tends to be in the form of tough love or absolute protection.

QUESTION 2 | DECISION-MAKING
When you make decisions, do you trust your head, your heart or your gut?

Listen for this

Type 2 | 2s generally say they follow their hearts when making decisions, particularly the tough ones. Although they may use their minds and guts, their hearts weigh larger in decision-making, in terms of values, impact on people, and more.

Type 8 | 8s make almost all their decisions from their instinctual center or gut. They've been doing it so long that it seems natural to them. In addition, their guts are more often accurate than inaccurate, so 8s have learned to trust it.

Some 8s may use their heads and hearts as well, but 8s perceive themselves as excellent, quick decision-makers, and most of it is from their guts.

> **QUESTION 3 | ANGER**
> How would you describe anger, how often do you feel it, and how do you express it?

Listen for this

Type 2 | Most 2s don't get angry all that much, but when they do, they can get explosive like a geyser because this emotion – as well as other feelings – tends to be repressed until it boils over and then gets outwardly expressed. After 2s express anger, they often feel relieved from the pressure, but anxious about losing control of themselves or embarrassed that they exploded in that way. The exception would be low self-mastery 2s, who feel and express explosive anger quite regularly.

Type 8 | Almost all 8s, unless they have been abused at an early age, perceive anger as simply energy and passion that they need to express. And once it is expressed, the anger is over and they move on to something else, although they may seek revenge later. In contrast to 2s, 8s rarely feel remorseful or guilty about feeling angry or expressing anger unless they have unintentionally hurt someone they care deeply about.

- Riding a bike -

TYPE 2 VERSUS TYPE 8

The confusion between type 2 and type 9 is one of the most common, and there are many reasons for this. Even though 2s are a Heart Center type and 9s are a Body Center type, 9s can be very heartfelt, people-oriented, and relational, much like 2s. In addition, both 2s and 9s are part of the "optimistic triad" – along with Enneagram 7s – so both 2s and 9s smile quite a lot and are adept at interactions that cause others to feel good.

QUESTION 1 | BEING LIKED
If you were to be completely honest, do you think you can get almost anyone you want to like you, or do you not think much about getting others to like you?

Listen for this

Type 2 | 2s, if they are willing to be honest with you, will admit they really can get almost anyone to like them. It is important to understand that 2s may not want everyone to like them, so they may not exhibit this "talent" all the time. But the skill is there. This question is best asked privately, however, because 2s may not want to admit this in a public forum!

Type 9 | 9s just usually draw a blank to this question and don't know how to answer it. That's because they don't think about it very much. After all, 9s are seeking harmony, connection, and rapport, not seeking for others to like them.

QUESTION 2 | FRIENDS
Would you please describe what "friends" means to you, the role they play in your life, and how you would describe them?

Listen for this

Type 2 | 2s almost always have a lot to say about friends, even multiple paragraphs. This is because they think about friends a lot. They will often describe having circles of friends that they have in categories, such as old friends and new ones; friends from this era and friends from that era; friends with whom they are close and those less so, and so forth. Friends are also people to whom 2s enjoy giving gifts without being asked to do so. Figuring out what friends like gives 2s great pleasure. Receiving gifts can be more challenging.

Type 9 | 9s don't usually have much to say about friends, and rarely do they have "circles of friends" with labels for their circles. This doesn't mean that 9s don't have friends or that friends don't matter; it simply means that thinking about friends in such detail is not really on their minds that much. In terms of gifts, 9s like to be given suggestions about what friends might want rather than to guess, and they relish receiving thoughtful gifts, such as something that might add to their collections.

QUESTION 3 | KNOWING WHAT OTHERS WANT AND NEED
Are you good at knowing and meeting others' needs, and how do you know what others need?

Listen for this

Type 2 | 2s say yes, knowing what others need and meeting these needs is second nature to them. How do they do this? 2s will say it is really intuitive, and if you ask about where this comes from, they will typically say from their heart area or say they pay a lot of close attention to people and remember what they've noticed.

Type 9 | 9s are usually not sure if they are good at this. They like to think that they are, but just aren't sure if they really are. When asked how they know what others need, they'll often say they'll ask the other person. 2s, by contrast, don't usually ask because 2s think they already know.

- Giving versus receiving gifts -

TYPE 2 VERSUS TYPE 9

TYPE 3 VERSUS TYPE 4

The confusion between type 3 and type 4 can occur for a few reasons. Both 3s and 4s are Enneagram types formed in the Heart Center of Intelligence and they are wings of one another. As a result, a person could be a type 3 with a 4 wing or a type 4 with a 3 wing. The type confusions can have to do with type and gender. Because 3s create an image of how they want to be perceived, if, for example, a 3 wants to appear to be sensitive, emotional, and artistic, the 3 may adopt more of a 4-like persona. By contrast, if a male 4 perceives his type as too full of feelings in terms of his cultural or familial context regarding how "males" should be and act, he might unconsciously start to use more of his 3 wing.

QUESTION 1 | IMAGE

Do you have a self-image of being competent, successful and confident, or is your image more about being different, unique, and not like other people?

Listen for this

Type 3 | 3s are about being competent, successful and confident, and they have many ways in which they know how to create this impression. For example, they breathe into their upper chest, even when feeling anxious; they talk about their accomplishments, some blatantly and some more subtly. Self-preservation subtype 3s might not relate to a question about image – this version of 3 has an image of no image – so listen for this. If someone says they have no image and that they are simply a very authentic person, they might be a self-preserving 3. In this case, ask them if they relate to being deep and emotionally expressive to get a sense if type 4 is a better fit. Most self-preserving 3s do not perceive themselves as highly introspective, for example.

Type 4 | 4s want to express themselves, particularly their feelings or their take on the world; being perceived as competent and successful is not a core value or issue for them. However, being perceived as deep, special, different, expressive and unique does matter to them a great deal.

QUESTION 2 | MOTIVATION

What motivates you more: getting concrete and clear results by setting specific goals and targets along with practical, concrete plans to achieve these, or deeply understanding and expressing yourself and connecting deeply with others?

Listen for this

Type 3 | 3s are motivated by concrete results, specific achievements, and continuously setting goals that are doable – often more than one goal, but not more than can be achieved. Normally, these are not highly detailed plans to accomplish their goals, but the plans are highly practical and concrete. Without specific goals and plans, 3s tend to feel lost and disoriented.

Type 4 | 4s are not driven by specific, tangible targets; they are motivated by deeper purpose, meaning and values. Although they can and do develop plans, the constant planning for achieving precise targets does not excite them. Instead, they prefer more lofty aspirations and deeper intentions to fuel their motivation, but will break these down into smaller milestones along the way.

QUESTION 3 | EMOTIONS

Would you describe yourself as a person who tends to keep most emotions at a lower volume level and only deal with them when necessary – and even then, for short periods of time – or as someone who values and invites deep emotions, both yours and those of others?

Listen for this

Type 3 | Almost all 3s push feelings aside, preferring not to deal with them as they arise. For 3s, feelings distract from getting work done. In fact, most 3s increase their activity as a way of not dealing with their feelings. In addition, they do not generally want to engage in emotional discussions with others as they are not used to it; emotional conversations can make 3s feel anxious; and diving into emotions can cause 3s to become distracted from pursuing their goals and plans.

Type 4 | Most 4s are highly introspective and exploring the intricacies of their own emotions and having these kinds of deep conversations with others feels real and satisfying. The exception would be the following: (1) a 4 might feel so overwhelmed with feelings that he or she retreats into a "cave" for a while, perhaps even becoming numb; or (2) some 4s can become highly and overly-analytical when they become emotional instead of experiencing their feelings deeply. However, even these 4s do enjoy most daily emotional interchanges.

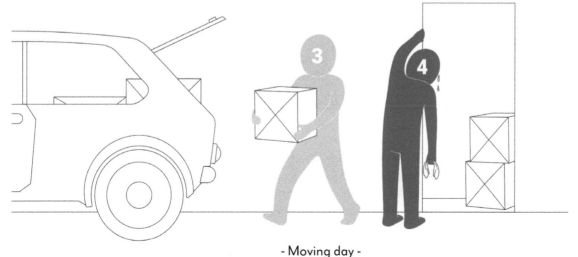

- Moving day -

TYPE 3 VERSUS TYPE 4

The confusion between type 3 and type 5 happens reasonably often for several reasons. Both 3s and 5s are Enneagram types that comprise the "competency triad" – types 1, 3 and 5 – meaning it is central to 1s, 3s and 5s to both view themselves and be perceived by others as competent. Next, some 3s may have an image of being intellectual and may want to be perceived as a 5. Third, although 3s are formed from the Heart Center of Intelligence, most 3s put aside their feelings in order to pursue goals and activity; this can appear to them to be the emotional disconnection of type 5. Finally, more introverted 3s may mistype themselves as 5s, but 5s are more withdrawn energetically, not just introverted. As you can infer from the above, it is more common for some 3s to think they are 5s than for 5s to mistype themselves as 3s.

QUESTION 1 | COMPETENCE
Is your sense of competence more about results and what you can achieve, or more about what you know?

Listen for this

Type 3 | For 3s, competence is about getting results, achieving concrete objectives, and being acknowledged for knowing how and being able to get things done. Think of this as practical, "can-do" competence. 3s like to get things done in a clear way, moving tactically and efficiently from point A to point B.

Type 5 | For 5s, competence is about their knowledge, insight, and understanding. Sometimes, they enjoy knowing about something just for the sake of knowing. Think of this as intellectual or mental competence. 5s like to research, consider, and strategize before taking action.

QUESTION 2 | FEELINGS
How would you describe the way in which you relate to your feelings and those of others: prefer not to feel too many emotions when you have work to do – which is most of the time – or completely disconnect from them in real time, but pursue some emotions later on when you are by yourself and do not have to engage with anyone else?

Listen for this

Type 3 | 3s do allow themselves to experience some feelings in real time, but also push them aside, if they can, to continue working or being active. However, pushing feelings aside is different from completely disconnecting from them, which is what 5s do. 3s also do not like prolonged emotional discussions with others. However, they will have some emotional conversations in real time, but for a short duration. 3s like the problem to be "fixed" and to move on quickly.

Type 5 | Most 5s, unless they have engaged in their own development for quite a long time, find the question about feelings to befuddle them. Sometimes they'll look perplexed, sometimes they may offer a statement about feelings that diminishes their importance. The area to listen for is whether or not the person says something like *Feelings are subjective* or *I only deal with them when I have to.* Ask specifically whether the person completely disconnects with their emotions – neither feeling them energetically or somatically – at the time they are occurring and then goes off later, to be alone, to relive some of them. This can be hours, days or months later.

QUESTION 3 | SOCIAL SKILLS

Would you describe yourself as a person who has strong social skills who can easily adjust to the person with whom you are interacting, or are interpersonal interactions challenging and draining for you, an arena where you have to expend a great deal of energy into making them work well?

Listen for this

Type 3 | Most 3s, including even introverted 3s, are adept at social interactions. Often called the "chameleons" of the Enneagram, 3s readily adjust their topics, delivery and communication to the person or persons with whom they are interacting.

Type 5 | Most social interactions demand a great deal of energy from 5s, unless the 5 knows the other person very, very well. And even then, if interpersonal conversations go on too long, 5s will need to take a break and create some space for themselves to recharge their energetic batteries.

- Playing a board game -

TYPE 3 VERSUS TYPE 5

The confusion between type 3 and type 6 can happen. 3s and 6s are on arrow lines to one another, so there may be some aspects of type 6 in every 3 and some qualities of 3 in every 6. In addition, the self-preserving subtype 3 is called "security," and these 3s are sometimes more visibly anxious (and aware of it) than are the other two subtypes of 3. This can make self-preservation subtype 3s wonder if they might not be 6s rather than 3s.

QUESTION 1 | RESULTS OR PLANNING
Do you like results more than planning or planning more than results? And even if you like both, if you had to choose which generates more excitement in you, would it be results or planning?

Listen for this

Type 3 | For 3s, the result is central, while the plan is a means to that end. So 3s will almost always light up about getting a positive result they intended. They also like plans, but the result is their end goal; the plan is the means toward the goal.

Type 6 | For 6s, the result is important, but the planning process is what engages and energizes them. They like to figure out contingencies, construct different pathways, and anticipate obstacles as a way to generate alternatives to overcoming potential challenges.

QUESTION 2 | FEELINGS AND ANXIETY
Do you tend to not feel your feelings that much on a daily basis and, in particular, bypass anxieties you might have by breathing into your upper chest and acting confident, or do you normally have an array of feelings, particularly anxiety or concerns as well as other emotions?

Listen for this

Type 3 | 3s do not like feeling emotions too often or too deeply, as they perceive feelings, both theirs and others, as more of a distraction from getting things done. Anxiety is particularly troubling for 3s, since they view anxiety as the opposite of – and an obstacle to – their displays of confidence. 3s, in general, push their feelings to the side, even though they are a type formed in the Heart Center of Intelligence.

Type 6 | Most 6s are more emotionally intense than most 3s because their heads spin round with concerns or creative problem solving, depending on their subtype and other factors. All 6s – even the highly counterphobic 6s who deal with feelings, and particularly anxiety, by going straight into risky behavior to prove they are fearless – are intense emotionally and their feelings and thoughts become so intertwined they may have difficulty separating them.

QUESTION 3 | PLANNING AND OBSTACLES

When facing a challenge, do you focus on creating an effective and efficient plan to reach your goals and get results, or do you focus on developing multiple pathways to achieve the result that take into account a wide variety of potential obstacles and contingencies?

Listen for this

Type 3 | Most 3s develop plans easily to achieve their endgame, but they tend to make them straightforward, relatively complete, and assume there will not be many obstacles. When obstacles arise, 3s can become perplexed or frustrated, especially when the issue isn't resolved quickly or easily.

Type 6 | 6s are idealistic realists who expect that obstacles will appear on the path to the end goal, anticipate these impediments as part of their planning, and then develop either multiple plans or one main plan with several alternative contingency arrangements. Figuring all this out excites them, although it can also unnerve them.

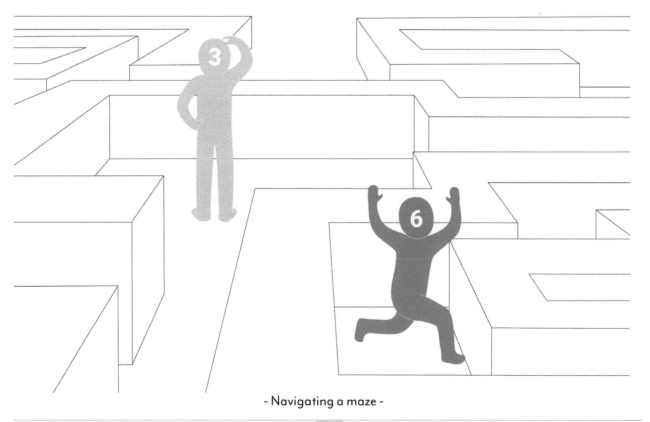

- Navigating a maze -

TYPE 3 VERSUS TYPE 6

Enneagram 3s and 7s are among the most common "look-alikes" of the nine types, so it is not unusual for many 3s to think they are 7s or 7s to think they are 3s, at least initially. They do have a lot in common on the surface. Both types are forward moving, energetic (although 7s are more so), positive in outlook (although 7s are more so), and get bored easily and don't like that feeling (although 7s are more so). Both 3s and 7s also "plan," but very differently. In addition, both 3s and 7s like to multi-task, but 3s set limits to the number of tasks they will take on, while 7s multi-task to an extreme and have trouble turning down anything that excites them. To help people sort through whether they are 3s or 7s, it is necessary to go beneath the surface, beyond behavior and into what drives the behavior.

QUESTION 1 | FOCUS
How long can you focus without extreme effort: as long as it takes to get the job done, or not very long because your mind wanders and you have to then put a lot of effort into staying focused?

Listen for this

Type 3 | For 3s, focus comes very easily because they set their attention on a specific goal or target and then stay with it until the job is done. They have almost a laser focus on projects they need to complete. Mission accomplished!

Type 7 | For 7s, focus is a challenge for them because they get easily distracted by new possibilities, thoughts streaming through their minds, external stimuli, and other factors. Some 7s will say they are focused, but it is important to ask them for how long and whether or not staying focused requires a great deal of effort.

QUESTION 2 | PLANNING
Do you go into practical planning mode quite easily when there is something you want to accomplish, or is your way of planning more about ideas in your mind, without necessarily a specific, pragmatic call to action that will take you from initiation to completion?

Listen for this

Type 3 | 3s are known for having goals and immediate, actionable plans. They may not write down their goals and plans because if it is not a complex task, there is no need for them to do so. Without goals and plans, most 3s feel highly disoriented.

Type 7 | When 7s plan, it is primarily about ideas and lots of them. Executing these plans, on the other hand, is usually something 7s would prefer others to do. Practical, pragmatic and detailed planning is not what most 7s enjoy or like to spend their time doing.

QUESTION 3 | OPTIONS AND MULTI-TASKING

Although you likely like to have options and enjoy multi-tasking, how many options do you really want and need?

Listen for this

Type 3 | Most 3s like options, but within limits. With too many options, it is hard for them to get the results they want. Doing everything can lead to getting very little done, and 3s love to get things done.

Type 7 | 7s want unlimited options; otherwise, they feel boxed in. In this way, having their options limited feels like an immense loss of freedom, and freedom is a necessity in their lives.

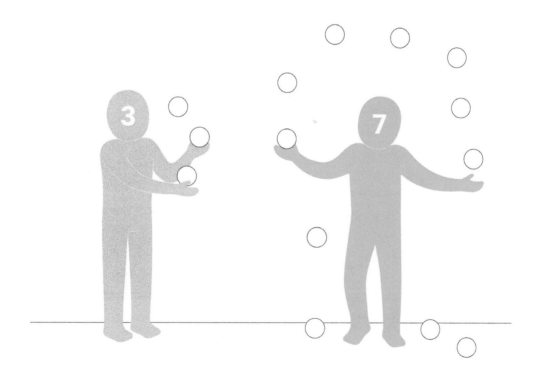

- Juggling -

Some Enneagram 3s may, at least initially, think they are 8s, but the opposite is less common. In other words, if 8s think they are 3s, it doesn't take very long to discover that they are not. The main reason for this particular type confusion is that both 3s and 8s appear to be confident, and both like to get things done. In addition, both 3s and 8s like to be respected, although 3s think they have to earn respect through their accomplishments, and 8s most simply expect it. In addition, both 3s and 8s get very agitated when they feel they have been disrespected.

Adding more to this type confusion, if a 3 has had a strong parental figure who was an 8, the 3 may be more asserting (more 8-like). In addition, 3s who want to be perceived as strong and bold may want to think of themselves as an 8 rather than a 3 and even start to act like one. Even more, 3s also imitate role models they admire, so if a 3 has had a type 8 role model, even as an adult, the 3 may start to act more like an 8.

QUESTION 1 | CARING WHAT OTHERS THINK
Do you care what others think of you and what you do, or do you really not care very much?

Listen for this

Type 3 | 3s care very much, even too much, about what others think of them and how they are perceived. They are attuned to reading the "audience" reaction, then adjusting what they do or say in response.

Type 8 | 8s care very little – although they sometimes care to some degree – about what others think of them or about what they do. In the view of 8s, they do what needs to be done; if people don't like it or are displeased, the action taken was still necessary. As a result, 8s rarely fret over how others perceive them unless they are very close to these people.

QUESTION 2 | PRACTICAL RESULTS OR HUGE RESULTS
Do you get energized and enthused by really good-to-great results no matter whether the effort is big or small, or do you need the results achieved to be very big and with a large impact to feel energized and enthused?

Listen for this

Type 3 | 3s don't mind big results at all, but they also get a great deal of satisfaction from getting positive results from their efforts, big or small. From their point of view, a good result is a good result.

Type 8 | From the 8 perspective, results need to be big in scope and bigger in impact. They don't like to bother with smaller tasks and items. Sometimes they think: *Go big or go home.*

QUESTION 3 | CONFORMING OR REBELLIOUS

Would you describe yourself as someone who accurately reads what is required and expected in different situations and then is adept at adjusting to the context you are in, or are you someone who is more rebellious and enjoys pushing against social expectations and norms?

Listen for this

Type 3 | Although many 3s would not describe themselves as conformists – and many 3s have some streak of inner rebellion – they do like to know what is expected and then meet or exceed that expectation. After all, that is what, in their minds, contributes to their success. In addition, 3s don't like to get in trouble with or push too hard against authority figures or rules if doing so will get them into trouble. In general, 3s like to know what the rules are and then play by them.

Type 8 | 8s often say they were born to be rebels, to break the rules, and to make the rules rather than to live by pre-established modes of conduct. Being rebellious in this way energizes them.

- Making something happen -

TYPE 3 VERSUS TYPE 8

Because 3s and 9s are connected by an arrow, many 3s feel familiar with aspects of 9 and vice versa. For example, when 3s get quite stressed, they may move to some qualities of type 9 and engage in a distracting activity to relax them such as video games, watching TV, or whatever takes minimal effort. And some 9s, particularly social subtype 9s, can get very active on behalf of groups or teams as they attempt to merge with a group or with work as a way to fit in or belong to the group.

In addition, some 3s appear mellow and relaxed, like 9s. However, this at-ease demeanor in 3s is more a result of their attempt to create a "cool" image and to not appear as driven as they actually feel inside.

QUESTION 1 | RELAXATION
Do you have difficulty truly relaxing and often feel more comfortable working under some degree of pressure (specific deadlines, for example), or do you relax very easily and more pressure makes you feel stressed?

Listen for this

Type 3 | 3s have difficulty relaxing, often perceiving relaxing as doing nothing, which for 3s is not OK. From the 3 perspective, their value is based on activity and doing something. 3s might relax by engaging in sports, but this is still an activity. In addition, some pressure gets 3s moving forward.

Type 9 | 9s love to relax and go into a zone of comfort of no pressure. They even do this when they "should" be doing something else. The tendency to engage in relaxing or non-essential activity is a regular occurrence for 9s, especially when faced with conflict, tasks they are concerned they may not be able to do, or pressure. Pressure to 9s feels like a demand or a form of control by others, and they don't like it at all, though they are unlikely to express this directly.

QUESTION 2 | READING AN AUDIENCE
Are you really good at reading your audience and then, if needed, adjusting how you look, act, and communicate to get the result you want, or do you not pay much attention to how you are coming across to others, preferring to just be yourself and engage with people?

Listen for this

Type 3 | 3s are highly adept at reading their audience, whether it be one other person, a small group or a large audience. They use their Heart Center to read how others are responding and then, often unconsciously, adjust their voice tone, what they are talking about, their physical demeanor and more in order to create a positive impression or impact.

Type 9 | 9s don't bother much to read their audience because this is not how they relate to others. Although 9s are usually very relational, they develop relationships by establishing rapport via small but interesting chats, blending energetically with the other person, or simply by being highly approachable and drawing others toward them.

QUESTION 3 | SPEEDY ACTION
Do you like to make things happen and to see concrete results quickly, or do you prefer to allow things to roll out smoothly in the best possible way, whether it takes a long time or very little time?

Listen for this

Type 3 | 3s really like forward movement and rapid action; in fact, they strive for this and become impatient when they perceive something as taking too long. They like results, they like them fast, and then they want to move forward.

Type 9 | 9s are fine whether something is fast, slow, or something in between, as long as it feels like something is happening and the outcome is going to be a positive one. When they feel forced to engage in speedy action, many 9s will resist, perceiving this as an unnecessary demand on them, even if they set the deadline themselves.

- Relaxing at the beach -

TYPE 4 VERSUS TYPE 5

Type 4s and 5s sit right next to one another on the Enneagram symbol, and if you visualize their placement on the circle, they are at the bottom of the Enneagram circle with an empty space in between. One reason for this placement is that these two type numbers look almost as if they could fall from the symbol, except that they are held together by the circle itself. There are no other lines between them. One way of understanding this is these two types are the most familiar with a sense of feeling isolated or separated from others. It is sometimes said about them that 4s represent "wet abandonment;" 5s represent "dry abandonment." In other words, 4s feel abandoned, know this, and feel sad in response. 5s, by contrast, sense this abandonment but are more stoic about it; hence, no tears from the 5s who detach from feelings automatically.

QUESTION 1 | EMOTIONS
Are you aware in real time when you are feeling emotional and do you also experience these emotions in your body, or do you rarely feel emotional in real time, but may realize and process what you are feeling later?

Listen for this

Type 4 | 4s are the most emotional of the nine Enneagram types, and they typically feel a myriad of emotions on a regular basis. They may go off later to analyze and process their feelings more, but they are not emotionally disconnected in real time.

Type 5 | 5s automatically and habitually disconnect from their emotions in real time, then go off later – which might be minutes, hours, days or months – and re-experience some of what they felt in a previous time. 5s also get confused about what is a feeling and what is a thought. Part of this is because to disconnect emotionally, they also disconnect somatically. And because feelings also have a physical or somatic sensation, many 5s do not have the somatic anchor by which to recognize and differentiate their emotional states.

QUESTION 2 | RESPONSES OF OTHER PEOPLE
Are you tuned into and care a lot about how other people are reacting to you, or do you not pay much attention to the responses of others and, if you perceive someone is upset with you, are you able to let it go fairly easily?

Listen for this

Type 4 | 4s are highly tuned into how others are responding to them, hoping for connection and affirming responses and wanting to avoid a sense of being rejected by others. Because of this, 4s care a great deal about the reactions of others and have a hard time letting go of what the 4 perceives as a negative response from someone else.

Type 5 | 5s often don't pay a lot of attention to the reactions of others or if they do, they don't get distressed by a non-positive reaction. 5s normally just go about their day, without ruminating. If someone is upset with them, 5s generally only really care if they are especially close to that person.

QUESTION 3 | TRUSTING YOUR HEART OR YOUR MIND
What do you trust more, your feelings or your mind?

Listen for this

Type 4 | 4s trust their hearts, feelings and emotional states far more than they trust their minds (or their bodies, for that matter). In fact, many 4s trust their feelings to such a degree that they say and believe, *I am what I feel*. As a result, 4s prefer people, experiences and interactions that resonate with their hearts. For example, musically, 4s tend to like love songs and instruments like the piano or cello.

Type 5 | 5s are the opposite when it comes to feelings versus thoughts. 5s trust their thoughts and don't trust feelings much at all. Most 5s believe that feelings are subjective and, therefore, not to be trusted. On the other hand, 5s also believe that thoughts are logical and therefore, objective and worthy of trust. 5s often say this: *I am what I think*. As a result, 5s prefer people, experiences and things that stimulate and connect with their minds. For example, 5s often like jazz or classical music, especially classical pieces that use instruments like the flute.

- Playing music -

TYPE 4 VERSUS TYPE 5

Type 4s and 6s are very different, and most often, these two types do not cause confusion. And yet, sometimes they do. And when they do, here is why. 4s and 6s are both part of what is referred to as the "intensity" triad (types 4, 6 and 8), a grouping of the Enneagram types that has in common the tendency to come across as intense in their general demeanor and in the way they interact with others. Although 4s are intense emotionally and 6s are intense mentally, from the outside, it can appear as if both types are just very intense. In addition, when 4s become emotionally intense, their mental function also gets highly activated; similarly, when 6s become mentally intense, their emotions follow close behind.

The other reason these two types can be confused is that 4s engage in "emotional push pull" with others (particularly in close relationships), while 6s can move toward and then move away from others, not necessarily only with those with whom they are close. These behaviors can look quite similar from the outside.

QUESTION 1 | HEART OR HEAD
Do you relate to your experiences primarily from your heart and emotions, or from your head and thinking?

Listen for this

Type 4 | 4s relate to almost everything emotionally. They can, however, get into excessive mental processing, but this is primarily when they are trying to analyze uncomfortable feelings as a way to understand or make them have less impact.

Type 6 | 6s are thinking almost all the time, and when they are not, they often start thinking about thinking. In addition, while 6s do think about their feelings and analyze them, they pretty much think about everything. This makes it hard for them to relax, but they often enjoy the complexity of their own minds.

QUESTION 2 | DEEP OR COMPLEX
Do you perceive yourself and do others view you as more of a very deep person or more of a complex person?

Listen for this

Type 4 | 4s usually experience themselves as very deep, symbolic people – deep in feeling, thought, and nuance. Although they may also be complex, deep is a better description.

Type 6 | 6s may be deep, but they are more aptly described as complex and even complicated. They often consider every possibility and enjoy puzzles – for example, life puzzles or real ones in which they can figure out the many possibilities, how to navigate the best ones, and so on.

QUESTION 3 | FUN
What do you do for fun?

Listen for this

Type 4 | 4s can be very serious and intense, but they also really enjoy having fun and can get quite silly and playful. They may also find something that is deep, meaningful and inspirational as fun. 4s will likely have several answers to this question and will likely enjoy answering it.

Type 6 | 6s want to have fun, but most 6s will find this question perplexing and will have to think about it a great deal. Many 6s say they don't have much fun because it is hard for them to relax enough to go enjoy themselves without being fully prepared for various contingencies. Fun for fun's sake may not be in their vocabulary. Or 6s might say they read, think or watch serious TV shows or documentaries for fun. Some 6s may look at you and say, "Fun? What's that?"

- Reaching the top of the mountain -

Type 4s and 7s can be thought of as opposites. Type 7s run away from sorrow and pain almost more than anything else – limits are something they also avoid – while 4s move toward pain and suffering, both their own and that of others. So why do people sometimes confuse 7s with 4s when they are so different? There are two reasons for this.

First, one of the three versions of type 4, the self-preservation subtype, is sometimes called the "sunny" 4. These 4s suffer in silence so that their suffering is not obvious. The name for this subtype, "reckless/dauntless," describes the type of behavior they use to move away from their suffering – for example, by engaging in behaviors that have an element of risk or excitement to them. In this way, self-preservation subtype 4s often have interesting and stimulating things they have done in their past that could make them appear akin to the stimulation seeking 7s. The second reason is that when 7s do get more deeply connected to their inner pain and suffering, they dive deeply into the place of sorrow and can appear somewhat like 4s.

QUESTION 1 | SADNESS
Do you stay with feelings of sadness, even when you prefer to not feel this way, or do you constantly avoid feeling sad by staying stimulated and excited, through positive thinking or by future-oriented possibility planning?

Listen for this

Type 4 | 4s tend to like melancholy more than deep sadness, but they generally do not avoid being aware that they are sad and deal with it as best they can. In addition, 4s tend to live more in the sorrows or nostalgia of the past than the positive possibilities of the future.

Type 7 | 7s will almost always say that they do not like sadness and do not feel it very often or for very long. Once they say this, ask them to describe what they do when sadness does occur, and listen for matches to the question just asked – stimulation, excitement, positive possibility planning.

QUESTION 2 | HEART OR HEAD
How do you know things and make meaning from your experience – from your heart or from your head?

Listen for this

Type 4 | 4s almost always make meaning from the heart. Although they may use their heads secondarily, they do so to make meaning of their emotions, which puts them right back in the heart.

Type 7 | 7s process almost everything from their heads. They share ideas and listen to others through the energy field of thoughts and ideas, and they make sense of their worlds through their minds. Of course, they have feelings, but making meaning comes from their Head Center of Intelligence.

QUESTION 3 | DEEP IN MEANING OR LIGHT-HEARTED IN INTENTION
Would you describe yourself as a deep person or a light-hearted person? And how would others describe you if they had to choose?

Listen for this

Type 4 | 4s would rarely describe themselves as light-hearted and, in fact, few actually are. Almost all 4s are deep emotionally, and they spend a great deal of time engaged in introspection. Most others also perceive 4s in this way.

Type 7 | 7s might want to experience themselves as deep, but this is not usually the case unless the particular 7 has gone through an extremely difficult situation and stayed with and processed their feelings. Otherwise, 7s perceive themselves as more light-hearted, though no 7 wants to view him- or herself as superficial.

- A day in the park -

TYPE 4 VERSUS TYPE 7

Type 4s and 8s are very similar and very different. To be more precise, a specific subtype of 8, the one-to-one subtype, can look very much like the one-to-one subtype of type 4. The reason for this potential confusion is that one-to-one subtype 8s are highly emotional, just as one-to-one subtype 4s are, and both one-to-one subtype 8s and one-to-one subtype 4s can be highly territorial, possessive and competitive in relation to what they think and feel belongs to them. The other reason 4s and 8s can be confused is that both are part of the Enneagram "intensity" triad. This means that in general, 4s and 8s (along with 6s) tend to be more intense than the other Enneagram types.

QUESTION 1 | GETTING WHAT YOU WANT
Do you think you can't really have what you want, even though you may try, or do you believe you can go after and take whatever you desire?

Listen for this

Type 4 | 4s start from a place of anticipating that their desires will be frustrated. They may know what they want, but their operating assumption is that they usually can't have this. Some 4s desire something and get paralyzed instead of going after it, while other 4s may go after something aggressively, but often don't get what they want to their satisfaction.

Type 8 | 8s usually know what they want and believe they can simply go after it directly and take it. In other words, they expect to get their desires fulfilled and so they, in a sense, grab what they feel they need. Of course, they may not always get the object of desire or their need met, but more often they do.

QUESTION 2 | MAKING DECISIONS
When you make decisions, is it more from your heart or primarily from your gut?

Listen for this

Type 4 | 4s almost always make decisions from their heart – the Heart Center of Intelligence – and if they use a backup, it is usually their minds or Head Center of Intelligence. It is possible, but unlikely, that some 4s would say they make decisions from their guts, but if you ask more questions and upon more reflection on their part, 4s often say decisions come initially from their Heart Center.

Type 8 | 8s almost always say that they make decisions from their guts, and they are quite emphatic about this. Decision-making is something they pride themselves in doing swiftly and strongly. Like 4s, 8s might use their Head Center as a back-up, but most 8s don't use the Heart Center as a secondary center in decision-making.

QUESTION 3 | TUNING INTO OTHER PEOPLE

Do you tune into how others are responding to you and care about this, or do you not care much about it, even if you might be good at reading other people?

Listen for this

Type 4 | 4s are extraordinarily sensitive to the responses of others, even if they sometimes read these responses incorrectly. And 4s do care about the reactions of others a great deal and will admit this.

Type 8 | 8s can be excellent readers of other people, and some 8s are not. However, reading others is not a central pre-occupation with them. And most 8s, unless it is in their personal life or they are keen on developing another person, don't truly care nearly so much as 4s about what is occurring inside the psyches of other people.

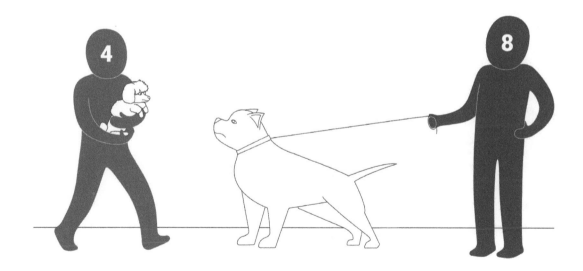

- Walking the dog -

TYPE 4 VERSUS TYPE 8

Enneagram types 4 and 9 don't usually cause confusion when people are trying to identify their Enneagram type accurately, but it does happen occasionally. The most common reason is when a 9 has a particular affinity for the more robust emotionality that goes with type 4. Because 9s merge with people with whom they feel an affinity – that is, they lose themselves in the energy of the person with whom they are merging – the 9 could mistake him- or herself for a 4 from having previously merged with other 4s.

QUESTION 1 | EMOTIONALITY
In your emotional life, even if you don't show it outwardly, are you highly intense and dynamic, or are you mellow and low key?

Listen for this

Type 4 | 4s, no matter what subtype, have an intense, dynamic, intricate, and robust interior emotional life. Some 4s express this externally, some keep their emotions more to themselves, and other 4s are a combination of external and internal expression of feeling. However, the emotional structure of 4s is the same: dynamic and intense.

Type 9 | 9s keep their emotions at a temperate range at almost all times, whether or not they express their feelings externally. In other words, 9s do experience a range of feelings, but most of their emotions are in the low intensity range. If, on occasion, 9s have more intense feelings, it often takes them a long time to recognize this.

QUESTION 2 | DEEP TALK OR SMALL TALK
When you engage with others in conversation, is your preference for – and are you adept at – deep, meaningful, and authentic conversations, or do you prefer and are adept at small talk or schmoozing in order to develop rapport?

Listen for this

Type 4 | 4s prefer the deepest and most real conversations possible, often getting bored or feeling ill at ease with small talk. When engaged in small talk, 4s often don't know what to say and have difficulty connecting with other people in this way. For example, 4s rarely take things as they are; instead, they relish the deep meaning and full experience of conversations and activities.

Type 9 | 9s are the masters of schmoozing. Most 9s can talk about almost anything for quite a while. Doing so relaxes them, puts them and others at ease, and establishes rapport. 9s can also engage authentically, but for the most part, they don't do so with great intensity. For example, 9s take things just as they are, taking pleasure in the comfort of conversations and activities they enjoy.

QUESTION 3 | LAMENTING OR BEING OPTIMISTIC
When something doesn't go as you'd hoped, do you lament about this in your conversations as a way to share your feelings, or do you keep your feelings more to yourself and turn to a more optimistic view of what has occurred?

Listen for this

Type 4 | 4s like to share their feelings, displeasures, and disappointments with others. Doing this helps 4s more clearly identify what they are experiencing, and it helps them to feel both supported and understood by others. Eventually, 4s may take a more optimistic perspective, but not initially.

Type 9 | 9s rarely lament when things don't turn out the way they'd hoped. They may talk about the situation with others, but they tend to do so more in a descriptive or optimistic way than in a lamenting manner. With something quite troubling, a 9 might lament internally, but rarely is this shared except with very close friends and family.

- Working in the garden -

© 2018 Ginger Lapid-Bogda PhD

TYPE 4 VERSUS TYPE 9

5s and 6s can cause confusion because both types are formed in the Head Center of Intelligence. As a result, both type 5 and 6 process their experience through thinking and planning, and both share the emotion of fear as a cornerstone of their types. In addition, 5s and 6s are directly next to one another on the Enneagram; hence, they are wings of each other. This means that there is likely a bit of type 5 in every type 6 and a bit of type 6 in every type 5. And if there is more than a "bit" – in other words, the wing is a strong wing – the confusion between these two types increases.

QUESTION 1 | DEALING WITH FEAR

Is your basic strategy for dealing with fear to withdraw, observe and strategize, taking action only when needed, or is it to think quickly and plan for all contingencies, sometimes taking action too quickly and sometimes too slowly?

Listen for this

Type 5 | 5s observe first and strategize second. In fact, they may observe and contemplate what is going on for a long time before acting. 5s are rarely prone to quick action, and they may act too slowly. In addition, they rarely plan for all contingencies.

Type 6 | 6s, when afraid – which happens quite often, particularly with self-preservation and social subtype 6s – go rapidly into multi-faceted thinking mode and ultra-contingency planning. The greater the fear, the more their heads spin. Sometimes they take fast action, sometimes their fast action is more impulsive than strategic, and sometimes they get paralyzed due to not knowing exactly what to do. One-to-one subtype 6s are especially prone to fast action.

QUESTION 2 | REMOTE OR INTENSE

Do you perceive yourself as a more remote person who doesn't generally show others what you are thinking and feeling, or are you more of an intense person who is easily "read" by others due to your verbal expressiveness and animated body language?

Listen for this

Type 5 | 5s are a "cool" enneatype that has perfected not showing to others what is going on with them internally. They can do this – that is, to not be transparent – because they are so private that they don't want anyone to know what they are thinking or feeling. It's known as a "poker face" that cannot be easily read. In addition, because 5s disconnect from their feelings in real time, unless they have done a great deal of development work, being opaque is relatively simple for them. There's not a lot to see in their non-verbal behavior, and 5s are deliberate in what they choose to share verbally.

Type 6 | 6s are usually highly intense, even if they sometimes think of themselves as more mellow than intense. When you ask them whether or not they are remote or intense, if they say remote, ask them what others would say about this.

QUESTION 3 | RELATIONSHIP WITH AUTHORITY FIGURES

With someone who is in authority, do you distrust them only if they have proven themselves untrustworthy and also have no expectation that they will keep you safe, or do you not really trust authority in general, but do expect them to keep you safe and secure?

Listen for this

Type 5 | 5s observe authority figures to try to figure out what they are going to do, but it is not a pre-occupation with them unless the 5 feels threatened or under siege. In addition, they certainly don't expect authority figures to keep them safe; 5s keep themselves safe by withdrawing and observing.

Type 6 | 6s watch authority figures closely and frequently in order to anticipate what authorities might do that could cause them or others harm. 6s also may try to befriend authority figures to show their loyalty so authority figures will be more likely to treat them well. 6s will also combat authority figures, particularly one-to-one subtype 6s, to prove their own strength and courage or to protect others. All 6s, to some degree, look to authority figures to keep them safe, while also believing authorities won't do so.

- Playing poker -

5s and 7s don't often cause confusion when people are trying to identify their types because the minds of 5s and 7s work so differently, and the ways in which they interact with others are distinctive. However, confusion can occur because both types are formed in the Head Center of Intelligence – and as a result, both have fear as the emotion driving their Ego structure – and they are on an arrow line with one another. This means that some 5s may also have some type 7 qualities and vice versa.

QUESTION 1 | HOW YOUR MIND WORKS

Does your mind work like a computer, with neatly organized files and files within files, so you can retrieve information of a similar nature, or is your mind more like a desktop containing every document as a separate file so you can make fast connections between things?

Listen for this

Type 5 | 5s have minds like a computer so that no matter how many files on it, there are files within files, within files, carefully organized for systematic retrieval. This also explains why 5s need to think about things before they talk; they're simply going into their retrieval system. 5s have logical, organized and clear minds, but not immediately fast retrieving minds unless they know something well. The 5 mind is called the "compartmentalizing" mind.

Type 7 | 7s have minds that are not particularly systematic or sequential. In fact, their minds are often described as "synthesizing" all kinds of seemingly unrelated data, making novel connections between things that the rest of us might not imagine. In addition, their minds move around from different ideas so quickly that, while they can follow their own way of thinking, others can find it challenging. It is as if every idea is a separate document on the desktop in their mind.

QUESTION 2 | DEALING WITH FEAR

When you feel fear, are you usually quite aware of it and what do you typically do in these cases, or are you less familiar with the emotion of fear and if you do experience it, what do you typically do?

Listen for this

Type 5 | 5s often say they are quite familiar with fear and may even give you examples. Because 5s tend to be thoughtful and introspective, they may also share nuanced versions of fear they experience, such as anxiety, trepidation, and more. Most typically, 5s will say that when they feel fearful, they step back, reflect, and strategize about how to deal with what they are feeling.

Type 7 | 7s may indicate that they do feel fear occasionally, yet many 7s will be surprised by this question and not know how to answer it. The reason for this is that when 7s feel fearful or anxious, they most often go into their minds and think about something else, usually something pleasant or positive. If that doesn't work, 7s will think about almost anything as an unconscious method to move away from fear. As a result, many 7s don't know how to answer questions about this emotion. They may even say that they never feel fearful.

QUESTION 3 | ENGAGING WITH OTHERS

How would you describe the way you tend to engage other people? Do you step back, observe, and then decide whether you want to engage with another person (and often prefer to not engage for extended periods of time), or do you move toward engagement with others and engage as long as you can with someone you find new and interesting until you get bored?

Listen for this

Type 5 | 5s step back and observe; they are sparing in their engagements with others unless they know the other person extremely well. Even then, 5s don't usually engage for indeterminate lengths of time because prolonged interactions feel energetically draining to them. 5s often want to know when the interaction will start, when it will end, and what is expected of them.

Type 7 | 7s are far more spontaneous in their interactions and will stay engaged for a long time if they are truly interested in the person and the topic. Many 7s find many people interesting, especially new people. 7s will bounce around from topic to topic, listen and talk almost at the same time, and they do all this in a highly animated manner.

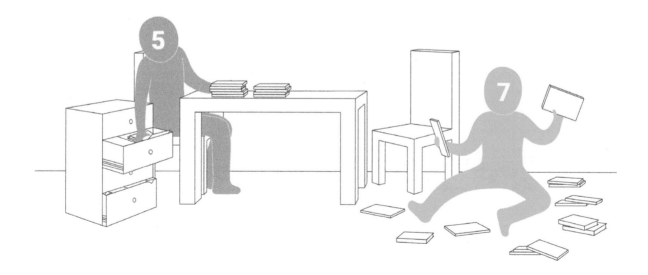

- Staying organized -

TYPE 5 VERSUS TYPE 7

5s and 8s are quite different from one another, yet there can be an occasional confusion between the two types. There are a few reasons for this potential confusion: (1) while 5s are a more withdrawing type and 8s are a more forward moving and assertive type, more introverted 8s may observe before they assert and sometimes be mistaken for a 5; (2) the self-preserving subtype 8 tends to be a quieter 8, checking out the scene for a variety of reasons such as assessing the power and influence dynamics or reserving their bigger energy for something that might come later and, thus, can be mistaken for a 5; or (3) a very angry 5, which does not happen that often, or a highly developed 5, who has much more access to his or her emotions and energy, might be mistaken for an 8. Types 5 and 8 are on an arrow line to one another, and as a result, there can be some 8ish qualities in every 5 and vice versa.

QUESTION 1 | PHYSICAL SPACE AND PERSONAL POWER
Do you take up less physical space and exert less personal power than you actually could, or do you take up a great deal of physical space and exert your personal power easily?

Listen for this

Type 5 | 5s minimize themselves, not wanting people to look at them for very long or to be the center of attention except under special circumstances. As a result, they take up less personal space than any other type, and they do not transmit a great deal of energy. 5s are generally the most self-contained of all the types. Even if 5s don't articulate that they take up minimal space – although most will because 5s tend to be introspective – other people can sense that there is more room for 5s to assert themselves energetically.

Type 8 | 8s take up a great deal of space and exert their energy even when they are being completely quiet. In this sense, their presence is felt in a room no matter what they are doing. In addition, 8s often maximize themselves, exerting their energy in order to take control of situations and to be heard.

QUESTION 2 | HEAD OR BODY
What do you trust more – for example, when making decisions or perceiving what is occurring – your mind or your gut?

Listen for this

Type 5 | 5s almost always say they trust their minds and logic. They almost never say they trust their hearts, primarily because they perceive emotions as illogical and unpredictable. And because most 5s, unless they have done a great deal of self-development work, are not very embodied, they often do not trust their somatic reactions either.

Type 8 | 8s trust their guts for just about everything – for example, decision-making, their perceptions of others, and their analyses of problems. It would be the rare 8 who would say he or she trusts the mind over the gut.

QUESTION 3 | ANGER
Do you more often have a delayed reaction to your emotional responses and then re-experience some of them later when you are alone and reflecting on your experiences, or when you experience emotions (and particularly anger), do you feel them intensely and in real time?

Listen for this

Type 5 | 5s are, more than any other type, habitually disconnected from their emotional states in real time. However, they often experience some of their emotions at a later point, which can be three hours, three days, or three months. Although 5s do get angry and may express this in real time if especially triggered, this immediate outward expression of anger is not that common.

Type 8 | 8s typically express anger quickly and often, even when they are trying to control its expression. Anger is the underlying emotion for the three types based in the Body Center of Intelligence (8s, 9s and 1s), and 8s are considered an "anger expressed" enneatype. However, 8s do not typically express other emotions such as sadness, anxiety or even joy, although this varies based on a number of factors, including subtype. The one-to-one subtype 8 is often emotionally expressive, although almost all 8s do not like to experience or express fear. When 8s feel fearful or vulnerable, they often get angry or take immediate, big action instead.

- Taking up space -

TYPE 5 VERSUS TYPE 8

TYPE 5 VERSUS TYPE 9

5s and 9s do, on occasion, get mistaken for one another, even though they are very different in Ego structure. This can come as a surprise to many who know the Enneagram, but it happens enough, particularly with a highly introverted 9. 5s and 9s show the least emotion of the nine enneatypes, and a highly introverted 9 may appear less accessible and more remote than most other 9s and slightly more 5ish.

In addition, social subtype 9s tend to be the most intellectual of the three subtypes of 9. Highly intellectual social subtype 9s – especially if they are more introverted – can have a very challenging experience sorting out whether they are 5s or 9s. And social subtype 5s, who connect with groups of people who share common values and interests and may work hard on behalf of this group can, initially, think of themselves as social subtype 9s rather than 5s.

QUESTION 1 | APPROACHABILITY
Do you set up strong, if invisible, boundaries so people sense when to approach you and how close they should get, or are you highly approachable with fluid interpersonal space and boundaries?

Listen for this

Type 5 | 5s set up strong interpersonal boundaries. In fact, they need far more physical distance between themselves and others than do any other of the Enneagram types. People don't normally approach them or touch them without first asking. Or if they do, 5s will either move away physically or their non-verbal behavior will indicate that the person has come too close.

Type 9 | 9s are the most approachable of all Enneagram types, and people often stand or sit close to them without hesitancy. For 9s, developing rapport is essential for a good relationship, and they enjoy merging or blending with other people, except those who complain frequently or seem very negative in some way.

QUESTION 2 | SCHMOOZING AND SMALL TALK
Does small talk or schmoozing feel annoying to you – and a waste of time – or do you enjoy talking with people about a variety of subjects in a relaxed manner as a way of establishing a relationship or developing rapport?

Listen for this

Type 5 | 5s almost always dislike small talk, perceiving it as having very little value. They are also not very good at it because they do it so infrequently.

Type 9 | 9s have developed their schmoozing skills to almost an art form. They don't actually perceive schmoozing as small talk because, for 9s, this way of conversing develops rapport in a non-threatening manner. It also relaxes them. Most 9s can talk about most topics in this manner, and if they can't, they still enjoy asking questions of the other person. For 9s, it's all about rapport.

QUESTION 3 | NO-NONSENSE OR RUDENESS
Do you perceive a short, direct response to a question as an effective no-nonsense way of responding, or do you perceive short, direct responses as blunt, non-relational, and even rude?

Listen for this

Type 5 | 5s get to the point when asked a question to which they have a clear answer. As a result, their responses are often short, direct, and on-point. Although 5s can talk at length about subjects they know a great deal about, with simple questions, they offer a simple and straightforward answer.

Type 9 | 9s do not particularly like short answers to questions as these can seem curt or even rude. From the 9 perspective, why not support positive engagement through pleasant conversation; the extra few minutes it might take are well worth the reward.

- Talking at the water cooler -

TYPE 5 VERSUS TYPE 9

6s and 7s are very different, but they can be mistaken for each other. Both 6s and 7s are formed in the Head Center of Intelligence and, thus, have fear as their common formative emotion; 6s respond to fear by being vigilant about themselves, others and their surroundings, while 7s run from their fear by pleasurable possibility thinking. 6s are idealistic realists who hope for the best and use planning as a way to remove obstacles to their desired intention, while 7s rarely think about what could go wrong. In addition, because these two types are wings of one another, 6s may have some qualities of 7 in them and vice versa.

QUESTION 1 | GLASS HALF-EMPTY OR HALF-FULL

When you plan, do you assume that the glass is half-empty – things can and will go wrong as in Murphy's law so you have to have back-up plans – or do you think and plan as if the glass is half-full, thinking that almost everything will work out and have a positive outcome, so you don't really need contingency plans?

Listen for this

Type 6 | 6s deeply want things to work out well, but they also are realistic and anticipate obstacles that might limit this. In this sense, they focus more on the half-empty and so create multiple contingency plans, just in case. They like to be prepared for various alternative realities.

Type 7 | 7s love ideas and possibilities and don't spend much time and energy on what could go wrong. In the 7's worldview, they believe that things just go well if you put your mind and attention to it. In this sense, their glass is almost always half-full, unless they are experiencing some difficult emotional states, which is quite rare, since they avoid these by thinking about something positive or becoming excited about something.

QUESTION 2 | INTROSPECTION

Do you perceive yourself as a reasonably introspective person, exploring and reflecting on your inner world of feelings and experience, or do you spend most of your time and attention thinking about new ideas and possibilities and engaging with interesting people and external stimuli that grab you in some way?

Listen for this

Type 6 | 6s are far more introspective than are 7s, and some 6s are deeply introspective, while other 6s are somewhat introspective. Also listen for sharing about concerns and anxieties, which is a fundamental part of the 6 inner world and which 6s pay far more attention to than do 7s, who are fear avoidant. The only subtlety about this distinction between 6s and 7s is that the more counterphobic 6s, who move to risky behavior when fear arises, may not talk about anxiety or fear because they take bold action when they feel anxious. However, they still tend to be more introspective than most 7s.

Type 7 | 7s are not nearly as introspective as 6s; 7s live in a more externalized world, noticing anything external that grabs their attention. This focus on the outside keeps them away from focusing on the inside. Some 7s do become introspective – and highly so – when they are in the throes of self-development work, so it might be important to ask someone who might be a 7 if he or she is going through an introspective period right now.

QUESTION 3 | FEELING RANGE AND DEPTH
Do you experience a wide variety of feelings and feel these intensely – for example, sadness, anxiety, anger, joy – or do you primarily feel joy and, occasionally, anxiety, anger and sorrow?

Listen for this

Type 6 | 6s are part of the "intensity triad" along with type 4 and type 8; they experience a variety of feelings and, as a result, people experience these three types as intense. Some 6s don't think of themselves as intense, although some do, so you may also need to ask the person who might be a 6 if others perceive them as intense. They may say, "I've heard this, but don't quite understand it." In addition, 6s do feel sadness, are generally familiar with anxiety – counterphobic 6s being a possible exception – and do get angry, although 6s tend to feel guilty when they do.

Type 7 | 7s are typically energetic, but not particularly intense. In fact, 7s have a "lightness of spirit," a quality which is the opposite of intensity. In terms of feelings, most 7s frequently experience positivity and joy, but rarely sadness. They can vary in terms of how often they feel angry or anxious.

- Playing tennis -

© 2018 Ginger Lapid-Bogda PhD

TYPE 6 VERSUS TYPE 7

6s and 8s are very different, except when it comes to the one-to-one subtype 6 and the 8 (all subtypes). 6s are a fear-based type, and self-preserving and social subtype 6s express their fear so that is easy for others to see. One-to-one subtype 6s go against their fear with direct action, often risky action, and can appear more fierce or strong than fearful. This physical and energetic strength of going straight into risky situations, combined with the fact that one-to-one subtype 6s are often more demonstrably angry than the other two subtypes of 6, can create a common case of mistaken identity with 8s. 8s are the Enneagram type most clearly expressing anger directly; the one-to-one subtype 6s can appear very similar in this way.

QUESTION 1 | DECISION-MAKING
Do you use your mind to figure out what to do in most situations, or do you use your gut?

Listen for this

Type 6 | 6s almost always say their minds, trying to find a logic to what might be the best alternative with the fewest downsides. This can be thought of as alternative pathing or mapping or as the development of alternative scenarios. Some 6s describe this as creative problem solving using multiple variables, and this can be very quick or take longer, depending on the complexity and seriousness of the issue at hand. Some 6s will say they use their guts, but this is usually only after their logical mind has explored the possibilities.

Type 8 | 8s come straight from the gut when making decisions. The process is fast and firm, and 8s usually trust the answer. Sometimes they are wrong, but they are right often enough to reinforce this way of decision-making.

QUESTION 2 | SUPPORT
Do you seek support from others and feel less anxious when you receive this, or do you rarely seek support from others, perceiving support as something you don't need and would not ask for?

Listen for this

Type 6 | 6s want support and may ask for it directly or indirectly, or they may non-verbally indicate they would like some. The core search for type 6, no matter what the person's subtype, is the quest for certainty, meaning and support. Self-preserving and social subtype 6s may look more in need of support than one-to-one subtype 6s, but even one-to-one subtype 6s, who tend to be the tougher and more counterphobic subtype, also seek out supportive individuals and groups.

Type 8 | 8s rarely admit they want or need support because they perceive this as a display of weakness and vulnerability. In addition, most 8s believe that most other people are not big enough or strong enough to support them anyway.

QUESTION 3 | VIGILANCE
Do you believe you must be constantly vigilant and alert, or do you take things more in stride, believing you can handle just about anything that comes your way?

Listen for this

Type 6 | 6s are constantly alert, almost as if their nervous systems are dialed up to full volume. This helps them feel prepared, but it also causes them to have difficulty relaxing. When vigilant, 6s can more readily perceive what is going on all around them; this includes front and back, top and bottom and side to side vigilance. This alert attention has somatic and emotional components, but more than anything, it is mental and strategic.

Type 8 | 8s are not particularly vigilant because they don't need to be. Rather than assuming that what can go wrong will or might go wrong – as 6s do – 8s assume they can handle just about anything that comes their way. As a result, there is no need for 8s to be constantly vigilant, with no need to get prepared in advance.

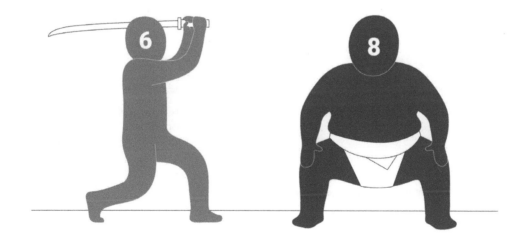

- Preferred martial art -

TYPE 6 VERSUS TYPE 8

6s and 9s are arrow lines of one another and, in this sense, there may be some elements of type 9 in every 6 and some aspects of type 6 in every 9. For example, 6s may enjoy nature to "space out" or relax, and 9s may be quite insightful and/or internally tense, although they tend to not share their insights outwardly and their internal tensions are often masked by a calm demeanor.

QUESTION 1 | TENSION OR RELAXATION
Are you finely tuned and tightly wired, or are you relaxed and very easy going?

Listen for this

Type 6 | 6s have an extraordinarily active nervous system from being on constant high alert. This causes them to be chronically tense and highly responsive to what occurs internally and externally. Some 6s may not be aware of being so tense because they have always been that way.

Type 9 | 9s take things as they come, they don't read that much into interactions or events, and they are the most relaxed and easy going of all nine Enneagram types. When they do feel tense, it rarely shows and they often don't recognize their tension until it builds up over time and becomes overwhelming.

QUESTION 2 | WARINESS OR OPENNESS
When you meet new people, do you tend to be more watchful and even wary while deciding if you can trust a person, or are you generally quite open and not cautious around new people?

Listen for this

Type 6 | 6s tend to have trust issues. Although some 6s might say they are too open initially, they are still calculating the risk of this trust and become distrustful quickly when they suspect someone is not being forthcoming, has a hidden agenda, or betrays their trust in some way. However, most 6s will say they do not trust people easily and are highly watchful regarding who they can and can't trust.

Type 9 | 9s don't concern themselves with issues related to trust, and they are neither watchful nor guarded with new people. Instead, they tend to like to talk, schmooze, and ask questions as a way to create comfortable relationships with others. Thus, 9s tend to be more open with new people than closed and more relational than guarded.

QUESTION 3 | INTENSE OR OPTIMISTIC

Would you describe yourself as an intense person – and would others describe you this way – or would you and others describe you as an optimistic person?

Listen for this

Type 6 | 6s are quite intense, even though they might not think of themselves this way. Some do and some don't. But asking about how others perceive them most often yields the answer: intense. The 6 intensity stems from a number of sources: their minds are constantly active as they anticipate and think through scenarios and potential problems to be solved; their emotions run through them continuously in response to what they are thinking, which is also constant; and they tend to move to action or inaction with a degree of fervency.

Type 9 | 9s are relaxed, calm, and optimistic, and tend to see the positive more than the negative. For these reasons, 9s are among the least intense of the Enneagram types. Their desire for collective harmony, their avoidance of conflict, and their lack of access to their own anger helps them stay optimistic and appear low intensity.

- Taking a swim -

TYPE 6 VERSUS TYPE 9

7s and 8s are wings of one another, and this is the most common reason for type confusion; a 7 can have an 8 wing and vice versa. In addition, both 7s and 8s are rebellious types, although they rebel for different reasons and in different ways. 7s rebel against limits of any kind; they believe they were born to be free with limitless possibilities in every direction. For 7s, rules of any kind are limits. 8s rebel against being controlled, unjust or arbitrary rules, and abuse of others. 8s also believe that rules are made to be broken. However, 8s don't mind rules if the rules make sense, and they like rules that they make themselves.

In addition, the passion or emotional pattern for 7s, gluttony, can be confused with the 8 passion of lust. However, gluttony causes 7s to constantly go after that which is new and stimulating; the lust of 8s, also called excessiveness, causes 8s to believe, "You can never get enough of a good thing."

QUESTION 1 | SPONTANEITY OR INTENSITY
Are you more fun-loving and spontaneous or more serious and intense?

Listen for this

Type 7 | 7s are fun-creating, fun-seeking, and spontaneous, searching for pleasure and avoiding life's difficulties if they can. Quite often, they believe it is their responsibility to keep everything and everyone up-beat and positive, and this can involve making jokes when serious issues arise or reframing something difficult into something positive and full of possibilities. In addition, although 7s are energetic, they are not particulary intense and rarely serious. In a sense, they crave stimulation through spontaneity and variety.

Type 8 | 8s are among the most serious of the nine Enneagram types, facing important issues directly and with intensity. In fact, 8s come across as intense even when they are saying very little. In a sense, they crave intensity through excessiveness. Their motto: *You can never get enough of a good thing!*

QUESTION 2 | HEAD OR BODY
Do you process most experiences through your mind or through you gut/body?

Listen for this

Type 7 | 7s, an Enneagram type formed in the Head Center of Intelligence, have minds that work like no other type on the Enneagram. Here is a brief summary of the 7's mind: (1) 7s have minds that process data so swiftly that others can hardly keep up with them; (2) the 7 mind connects, at least from the perspective of others, ideas that are not obviously related and then synthesizes them into innovative ways of thinking; and (3) the 7 mind moves to thoughts of pleasure and possibility instantaneously. As a result of their highly active minds and also because of it, 7s process almost everything through their minds.

Type 8 | 8s are the most body-oriented, gut-trusting of all the types, even more than 9s and 1s, the other two Enneagram types formed in the Body Center of Intelligence. 8s process almost everything through their bodies, and they trust their guts unequivocally in almost all situations.

QUESTION 3 | OPTIMISM OR REALISM
Do you think you are a more optimistic person or a more realistic person? Would others agree with this?

Listen for this

Type 7 | 7s are the most optimistic of the nine Enneagram types. They are wired to think of the positive and not the negative, to reframe potentially negative thoughts and experiences into positive ones, and almost always have a constant smile on their faces. Their motto: "Don't worry; be happy."

Type 8 | 8s are the most realistic of all nine Enneagram types. They live on solid ground, are strongly rooted, and value the idea that they deal with the real world in real time with real issues. Although some 8s can be optimistic at times, most 8s perceive constant optimism as not living in the real world. As a result, they tend to appear more serious, smiling only when something specific delights or pleases them.

- Devouring dessert -

TYPE 7 VERSUS TYPE 8

7s and 9s are sometimes confused with one another because both belong to the "optimistic triad," along with type 2. What this means is that 7s, 9s and 2s have the most optimistic or positive view of people and the world, with 7s being the most optimistic, 9s being the next most optimistic and 2s being less optimistic than 7s or 9s. Another way of understanding this is that these three types embellish reality more than the other types, perceiving things as better than they actually are. One way to think about the difference between 7s and 9s is this: 7s are energetic optimism; 9s are relaxed optimism.

QUESTION 1 | STORYTELLING
When you tell a story about something that has occurred, do you start in the middle where you are most excited, or do you start from the beginning and then share the story in sequence?

Listen for this

Type 7 | 7s are storytellers, but they rarely start at the beginning, preferring to begin with the part that most excites them and then move around the story to share the parts about which they are most enthused. As a result, 7s often don't know when to stop a story since they don't necessarily get to the end! They tell stories in a way that most energizes them.

Type 9 | 9s are also storytellers, but they tell them in a sequential way, starting at the beginning, then moving in sequence to the end. They do this for two main reasons. First, 9s believe that context is important for understanding a story, so they share the context of the story at the beginning. Second, 9s like to remember all parts of the story and going in sequence helps them to not leave anything out. Although the stories may feel long from the perspective of others, not so for the 9 storyteller.

QUESTION 2 | INTERRUPTIONS
How do you define an interruption when someone is talking? Is it when someone says "no" to an idea you have, or is it when someone says something while you or another person is speaking?

Listen for this

Type 7 | 7s rarely feel interrupted by others because they actually enjoy it when someone else comes in to interject a thought or build on an idea when the 7 is speaking. To 7s, this feels like engaged listening and interaction, not an interruption. This is called "overlapping" conversation. When 7s listen, they jump in the middle when someone else is talking because they are excited. 7s feel most interrupted when another person negates an idea the 7 has shared.

Type 9 | 9s do not like anyone coming in to say something before the 9 has completely finished a sentence, a thought, a concept or a paragraph. Not only do 9s perceive this as interrupting, they consider it rude, disrespectful, and diminishing. In addition, these interruptions often cause 9s to lose their train of thought and forget where they are in terms of what they are trying to communicate. 9s also listen without interrupting until the other person has finished, and then will add their own comments.

> ## QUESTION 3 | ATTENTION DIVERTED
> When your attention gets diverted, do you think about exciting ideas or engage in stimulating activities, or do you tend to go for activities that provide you with comfort and familiarity?

Listen for this

Type 7 | 7s get diverted quickly and often, and when they do, their minds move rapidly to interesting ideas, stimulating thoughts, future plans, or they engage in activities that excite them. This can happen hundreds of times per day, rather than being a behavior that happens occasionally and only under certain conditions. 7s automatically divert their attention when they are bored, excited, anxious, sad, and for a variety of other reasons.

Type 9 | 9s get diverted only under certain conditions: when they are anxious; when conflict looms and they are directly involved; when they are angry at someone or another person is angry at them; when they feel pressured to do something; and when they don't know how to do something. In addition, the 9s' diversionary tactics tend to be that which is familiar and comforting to them. For example, they may watch TV, read books, go for many long walks, do crossword puzzles, or add to one of their collections; most 9s have collections that they enjoy buying for themselves or receiving as gifts.

- A quiet day at the lake -

8s and 9s are wings of one another, and as a result, there can be some 9 qualities in many 8s and some 8 qualities in many 9s. They are also two of the three types formed in the Body Center of Intelligence, along with type 1 – all three Body Center types have issues with anger and control – which can make them seem similar.

QUESTION 1 | ANGER
When you get angry, do you tend to know you are angry and express it, or are you often not even aware you are angry and have difficulty expressing your anger when you do feel it?

Listen for this

Type 8 | 8s, at least most 8s, express their anger readily and often. They may say they don't get angry that often, but they mean that they don't get furious or rageful daily. However, they do feel other forms of anger quite frequently, such as annoyance, frustration, contempt, and more. In addition, when 8s feel any form of anger, they almost always are aware of it due to their familiarity with the corresponding somatic sensations in their bodies. And when they feel angry, 8s feel the need to express it directly. In this sense, 8s can be thought of as "anger expressed."

Type 9 | 9s often don't know that they are angry even when they are quite distressed. In their attempts to keep harmony and good-will, 9s unconsciously lose touch with their somatic experience and, as a result, don't really know whether they are angry or not. The emotion of anger starts as heat that grows in the base of the belly and intensifies as it moves upward, but 9s may not realize they are angry until the sensation becomes extraordinarily intense. In this sense, 9s can be thought of as "anger that went to sleep."

QUESTION 2 | CONTROL
With regards to control, do you like to feel and do you need to feel in control of situations at almost all times, or is your concern with control more that you just don't like other people controlling you?

Listen for this

Type 8 | 8s like to feel in control of just about everything for several reasons: (1) they feel it is their responsibility to keep and hold everything together; (2) they are highly attuned to chaos and lack of control, and feel a need to step in quickly when this happens; and (3) if everything is not under control, 8s feel vulnerable and as if everything is going to fall apart. For 8s, think of control as a constant need for strong, direct influence and impact.

Type 9 | 9s simply do not like others controlling them; few 9s express interest in controlling others and situations on an ongoing basis. Given their sensitivity to being controlled, many 9s feel controlled by things that would not generate the same reaction in other Enneagram types. For example, if a 9 is asked "Did you finish that project?" or "Did you take out the garbage?," many 9s will react to this as if the question is pressure on them, and pressure is the same as someone trying to control them.

QUESTION 3 | TAKING UP SPACE

Do you have a big presence – or at least are told often that you do – or do you tend to minimize yourself and not assert yourself very often?

Listen for this

Type 8 | 8s almost always have a big presence, even when they are silent, and they take up quite a bit of space, almost as if they "own" the territory. This is the result of their being more fully in their bodies than many other people, and it is also a way they assert themselves. 8s also tend to talk louder than most others, have more resonant voices, and they use direct eye contact and step forward when engaging with others. Verbally or non-verbally, 8s assert "I am here!"

Type 9 | 9s, by contrast, tend to minimize themselves, not call attention to themselves through their voice tone or dress style, and they tend not to speak up, at least not initially. It's not that they are passive, but they are rarely aggressive. Their existential position is something like this: "I don't really matter."

- Having an argument -

© 2018 Ginger Lapid-Bogda PhD

PART III

CHAPTER 4 | OTHER TYPING FACTORS

CHAPTER 4 | OTHER TYPING FACTORS

CURRENT CONTEXT **FACTORS**

Understanding a person's current context is important in helping that person identify his or her type accurately. Here are some common examples, along with what to consider and what you can ask.

Stress

A person undergoing a large degree of current stress and related anxiety may seem like a type 6, but stress can come from many contextual sources: work environment, finances, job security, children, elderly parents, and natural disasters.

ASK: Are you currently under a great deal of stress, more than normal? If the answer is *yes*, you don't need to know what the stress is – that is, no need to probe what is causing the stress unless the person volunteers this information. Simply ask this: *Without this current stress in your life, which type do you believe would fit you best?*

Sadness

A person who appears very sad currently may seem like a type 4, but sorrow can come from many contextual sources: death, divorce, job loss, relationships, and natural disasters.

ASK: Currently, are there factors in your life causing you to feel extremely sad, sadder than normal? If the answer is *yes*, you don't need to know what is causing the sadness – that is, no need to probe what is causing the sadness unless the person volunteers this information. Simply ask this: *Without this situation in your life causing the sadness, which type do you believe would fit you best?*

Anger

A person who appears very angry may seem like a type 8, but this person may simply be angry about something in his or her current situation or may be in touch with an old anger that has been suppressed, repressed or festering for years.

ASK: Currently, are there factors in your life causing you to feel more angry than you normally feel? If the answer is *yes*, you don't need to know what is causing the anger – that is, no need to probe what is causing the anger unless the person volunteers this information. Simply ask this: *Without this situation in your life causing the anger, which type do you believe would fit you best?*

Caregiving roles

People who have been or are currently in long-term caregiving roles may seem like a type 2. This can be the case when the long-term caregiving roles were from their youth – taking care of parents who were sick or impaired; taking care of siblings as a surrogate parent; or a family role assigned for a variety of reasons. These role-based behaviors often carry over into adulthood. Caregiving roles can also stem from adulthood – for example, taking care of spouses, siblings, parents or others in need of intensive caretaking for a variety of reasons. However, being in caretaking roles does not make a person a type 2.

ASK: *In your taking care of others, are there factors in your background or in your current situation that might have caused you to be a caregiver that were not necessarily your more natural orientation?* If the person gives an answer that makes sense, then ask this: *Without this situation causing you to be in the role of caretaker, which type do you believe would fit you best?*

PETER O'HANRAHAN

 As Enneagram teachers, we have our own biases, and we may be talking with someone during a period of big stress or big change in their lives; this can skew the result. It's best to say: 'What I hear in this conversation is... or it sounds a lot like this type, but there may be other possibilities for you to explore.'

Peter O'Hanrahan has been teaching the Enneagram for almost 40 years and is a senior trainer for Enneagram Studies in the Narrative Tradition.

OVERLAY FACTORS

Family overlays

There are many overlay factors that can influence a person's self-perception, as well as how they may appear on the outside in terms of behavior, appearance, and even their style of verbal or non-verbal behavior. Whether or not a family overlay is present depends on the degree to which an authority figure in the home had a pervasive influence on the family, not whether an authority figure of a certain type was present in the family. A dominant authority figure includes mothers, fathers, grandparents, and even older siblings. When this occurs, most, if not all, of the children in the family will have the same type overlay.

For example, if a type 1 family overlay exists, the children tend to be more perfectionistic, more critical, or more rule oriented than they might be normally. A type 2 overlay often creates a family system in which the offspring focus more on others than themselves, tend to give more gifts or feel guilty when doing things for themselves. A type 3 overlay might create siblings who are highly achievement-oriented and who feel they must constantly excel. A type 4 overlay in a family could create a cadre of aesthetically-oriented children or ones who are more sensitive and deeper than they might be normally. For a type 5 overlay, the family system might be cooler – for example, not-sharing of emotions readily – and more intellectual and private. For type 6, the family overlay depends on the parental subtype, but in general, this family overlay tends to be one in which children raise doubts more frequently – both internally and externally directed – and do more contingency planning. A type 7 family overlay influences the offspring to be more upbeat and interactive or at least believe that they should be this way. Type 8 overlays often generate families where the children present themselves as tougher or stronger than they actually are. Type 9 family overlays usually have children who are conflict averse, have more challenges expressing their anger, but who are also more easy-going and try to unite people.

Culture overlays

Not every country or culture has an easily identifiable Enneagram type or only one type, but some do such as France (type 4, likely a one-to-one subtype 4), Canada (type 9), and the US (type 3, likely a social subtype 3).

What does this mean in terms of typing? With many French people having a type 4 cultural overlay, they will tend toward the aesthetic and the symbolic, as well as be likely to engage in deep meaningful conversations. Think of all the French artists over the centuries, the abundance of art galleries, and the French past-time of having long conversations in sidewalk cafes, weather permitting. Without understanding French culture, people from France can get mistyped as 4s.

Canada (type 9) is known as one of the more inclusive of countries. Most Canadians are relatively easy-going and tend to get along well with other people, just like 9s. The US is made up of many subcultures – for example, Texas is more type

8-like and Maine is more type 5-like – but most people from the US have a type 3 overlay. In the US culture, Enneagram 3s get especially rewarded and the other eight Enneagram types tend to have a more short-term results orientation than they might have normally. Without understanding French, Canadian, and US cultures, people from these countries can get mistyped as 4s, 9s or 3s, respectively.

Gender-based overlays

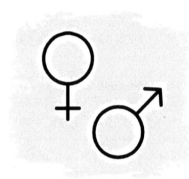

Gender-based overlays are culture specific and are connected to the expectations and stereotypes of women and men. Although all cultures have views of how men and women should be, look like and behave, in some cultures these are so strong that they can cause some confusions in typing.

One of my clients from South Korea told me this: "In South Korea, the men are expected to act like 8s and women are supposed to appear to be 9s." In the United States, some type 2 males and some type 4 males get told from their youngest years that they are too sensitive or too emotional. As they grew up, some type 2 males began to act more like 3s (a wing) or 8s (an arrow), while type 4 males may have adopted more qualities of 3 (a wing) or 5 (a wing).

In the US, many female 8s may not recognize themselves as 8s at first because the social conditioning for women has driven home this message to young female 8s: *Don't be so strong!* As a result, some female 8s from the US may have morphed into 9s (a wing) or 2s (an arrow line) to deal with this. Coming home to their 8ness can be a great relief.

Type-based overlays

Another kind of overlay can occur in all types. This occurs when a person truly admires another person to such an extent that they try to emulate that individual. A person, for example, may have admired a type 8 boss and then begins to act somewhat like an 8 when in a leadership role. This sort of type imitation is most common in type 3s who, by their type-based inclinations, seek out individuals – real, historic, from literature or even film – who appear to be successful and then try to imitate that person's attitude, behavior, voice tone, and more. When type 3s do this, they can get confused as to what is truly them and what has been internalized from another person. Even without having a concrete role model to imitate, some type 3s may have a self-image or a desired persona that fits more closely to another type. As a common example, a type 3 who wants to be perceived as intellectual may mistype him-or herself as a type 5. A type 3 who wants to be perceived as strong and bold may mistype him- or herself as a type 8.

LEVEL OF *SELF-MASTERY* FACTORS

A low self-mastery individual is relatively low in self-awareness and usually has a more difficult time accurately identifying his or her type easily. They may not have an accurate self-understanding, which hinders their capacity to objectively observe their own motivations and patterns of thought, feeling and behavior. All of this hampers their ability to find their type; it may just take them longer.

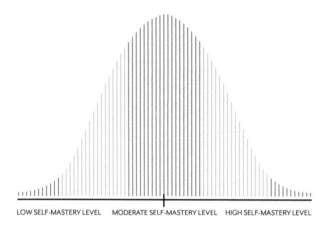

LOW SELF-MASTERY LEVEL   MODERATE SELF-MASTERY LEVEL   HIGH SELF-MASTERY LEVEL

High self-mastery individuals typically are easy to type if the person guiding them provides accurate information and allows the individual time to reflect. The issue with high self-mastery individuals, however, is that they have usually done so much self-development work that their type-based issues and behaviors may not be so obvious. For example, a type 5 who has become extremely integrated may not appear to be disconnected emotionally or out-of-touch somatically. Even asked if he or she automatically disconnects emotionally, the answer may be *no*. But if the question is followed up with *Did you used to do this and, if so, how often*, the person may see him- or herself very clearly in type 5.

WING AND ARROW FACTORS

Wings, the Enneagram types on each side of a person's actual Enneagram type, can provide secondary characteristics to our core type as can the two arrows – one pointing away from and one pointing toward our core Enneagram type. As a result, some people discovering their core type may be confused between their true type and a wing or an arrow. For example, a type 7 may not be sure if he or she is a type 7 or a type 8 (a wing of type 7), or if he or she is a type 7 or a type 5 (an arrow line of type 7). The differentiating questions in this book are ideal for people who want to discern between any combination of two types, including wings and arrows. Detailed information about wings and arrows is described in Appendix C.

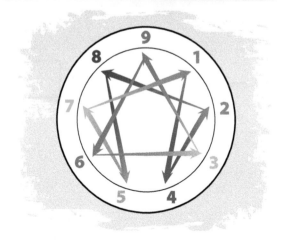

VERBAL AND NONVERBAL TYPING FACTORS

VERBAL CUES

Repeated use of judging words:
ought, should, right, wrong, must
Offer opinions frequently
Use precise language

NONVERBAL CUES

Tight jaws from withholding anger
Self-controlled bodies
Upright posture

VERBAL CUES

Ask frequent questions of others
Soft voice unless angry
Give compliments

NONVERBAL CUES

Shoulders rounded with slightly caved chests
Eyes make warm interpersonal contact
Smile as an invitation to engage

VERBAL CUES

Want to get to the point quickly
Logical, clear, concise speech
Give ideas in sets of 3 points

NONVERBAL CUES

Shoulders more horizontal than rounded
Energy in face and upper body
Confident demeanor

VERBAL AND NONVERBAL TYPING FACTORS

VERBAL CUES
Frequent sharing of personal stories
Frequent use of *me, my, mine,* and *I*
Deliberate word choice

NONVERBAL CUES
Appear focused inward
Wet or moist eyes
Intense

VERBAL CUES
Talk at length if knowledgeable
More often quiet than talkative
Use minimal language

NONVERBAL CUES
Eyes appear as if observing themselves
Self-contained body
Low animation

VERBAL CUES
Hesitant or highly assertive speech
Frequent use of *what if* questions
Use analytical language

NONVERBAL CUES
Darting eyes as if scanning
Hyper-vigilant demeanor
Appear tense or stressed

VERBAL AND NONVERBAL **TYPING FACTORS**

VERBAL CUES

Fast, spontaneous speech
Upbeat word choice
Tell engaging stories

NONVERBAL CUES

Bright, excited eyes
Smile continuously
Highly animated

VERBAL CUES

Use profanity or body-based humor
Short, simple sentences
Give commands

NONVERBAL CUES

Authoritative with strong physical presence
Grounded, almost immovable
Direct eye contact

VERBAL CUES

Give highly detailed information
Use agreeing words like *uh huh*
Share information in sequence
from first to last

NONVERBAL CUES

Minimal facial tension
Easygoing demeanor
Relaxed posture

SOMATIC INSIGHTS ON TYPING

Guide rather than tell. Watch their body language. What lights them up? What gives them a deep settling into inner peace? These are signals you can recognize, note and share with them, for their consideration. There's no hurry. The reflections and the inner work along the way have great value.

Andrea Isaacs, a global Enneagram teacher and Riso-Hudson faculty member since 1994, is the creator of the EQ Quiz, EnneaMotion, and Somatic Focusing, creating new neural pathways to increase Emotional Intelligence.

ANDREA ISAACS

I consider everything – what they say, how they say it, body language, physical appearance, and my internal reactions to them and their energy. After we narrow it down to their likely type, all the data needs to be congruent with that Ego structure. If not, I ask them to make sense of it. When they can, they've landed in the right place.

Matt Ahrens MBA is a psychotherapist, coach, trainer, consultant and an Internship Coach for the Enneagram Professional Training Program, and was past president of the Enneagram Association in the Narrative Tradition.

MATT AHRENS

As you engage in a typing conversation, listen with your 3 Centers of Intelligence – Head, Heart and Body – as well as your intuition. Notice when the person's energy seems to "pop," enlarge, and expand. When this happens, it often indicates that person's type.

Anne Mureé has been teaching the Enneagram for over 20 years, is a transformational coach and the author of the upcoming book, *Teaching the Enneagram with Mastery.*

ANNE MUREÉ

Keep your radar on for reflexive recoil. When someone is introduced to the system and has an adverse reaction to a particular type, take note. This could be rejection of characteristics the seeker doesn't want to own and an indicator of the person's type home base.

Monirah Womack is an organization consultant, coach, trainer and Enneagram teacher, and past president of the Enneagram Association in the Narrative Tradition.

MONIRAH WOMACK

APPENDIX

ADDITIONAL RESOURCES

APPENDIX A | TEACHING TYPE

There are many ways to teach the Enneagram system and to help others find their Enneagram type accurately. However, any method used requires the person teaching the Enneagram to know the Enneagram themselves in depth. The Resources section at the back of this book provides a list of books, websites, training tools, online tests, training programs and more that focus on enhancing typing skills.

MOST COMMON METHODS FOR TEACHING THE ENNEAGRAM

The most common methods include the following, accompanied by the pros and cons of each method: lectures, typing cards, interactive activities, type panels, typing interviews, and tests. These approaches are not mutually exclusive – that is, most Enneagram teachers, trainers and coaches use more than one approach, which is highly beneficial.

Lectures

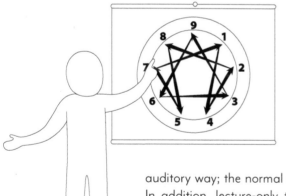

Lectures are effective if the trainer (1) knows the Enneagram well, (2) can explain the system and types to newcomers in a clear and accurate way, and (3) uses excellent teaching aids, such as PowerPoint slides, to support learning.

The issue when teaching through lecture only is that it requires that the trainer be an outstanding presenter who can maintain a level of excellence for an extended period of time – for example, 4-8 hours. In addition, a lecture-only method requires that participants are capable of absorbing material in a primarily auditory way; the normal attention span for lecture is somewhere between 15-30 minutes. In addition, lecture-only teaching offers only minimal assurance that a majority of the participants can identify their types accurately because there is little opportunity to verify type.

Typing cards

Typing cards are an effective typing method, and we provide two different sets of cards by which to do this: *Enneagram Typing Cards* and *The Enneagram Discovery Deck*, both of which are described below. Typing cards do not always give a definitive answer to type, but they do provide people with a kinesthetic way to consider certain types as more likely and to eliminate others. Other forms of typing cards are also available from other providers.

With both of my typing card options, people sort the cards into *Yes, No, Maybe*, then rank order their *Yes* pile from most *Yes* to least. Most people get their actual type in their *Yes* pile, often as #1 or #2. Most commonly, people find their type as their #1 card or among the top three cards. For this reason, and just as with all typing methods, the trainer or coach needs to know the Enneagram system and all nine types well enough to help the client differentiate between types because of "look-alikes," wings and arrows of a type, subtypes, and other factors.

The *Enneagram Typing Cards* are also available on an app, *Know Your Type*, created for iOS (Apple), Android and Kindle Fire platforms. The app, which has far more than only the animated typing cards, can be used with individuals or groups as long as each person has a smart phone or tablet.

Interactive activities

Interactive activities not only engage people, they give people a first-hand experience of themselves. This matters in typing because how people think they are – also called "self-report" – may not be how they actually are. This can be true even for people who are relatively self-aware. Examples might include a somatic exercise where participants are directed to move in space from each Center of Intelligence – Head, Heart, and Body – and to then understand the degree of access they have to each Center. Other exercises would need to follow – for example, belief systems of each type posted on a wall, with participants then moving to the belief system that most aligns with how they think. And then more exercises would need to be carefully stacked upon these.

To construct these kinds of interactive activities and make them effective in helping people identify type, it takes a very savvy instructional designer with deep knowledge of the Enneagram and top-notch facilitation skills to be able to process the exercises.

Type panels

Enneagram type panels are a group of people of the same type – usually 3-6 people – interviewed by a trained Enneagram facilitator who asks the panelists a set of exploratory questions related to that particular type. The facilitator's questions usually start out as general ones, after which the facilitator asks relevant probing questions related to the panelist's response. The audience learns about the types based on the "stories" of the panelists and tries to assess which type panel might be most similar to them.

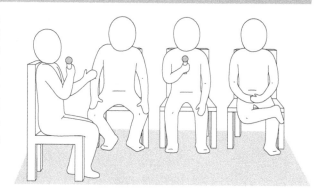

Type panels are an excellent way to teach Enneagram type, but the conditions need to be ideal. First, panels take time – at least 30-45 minutes per type panel – and because there are nine panels, teaching type by this method can take a minimum of two days. Second, effective type panels require that the panelists already know their type accurately. This is not possible if all participants are new to the Enneagram. Third, the group size must be large enough to get 27 panelists, three individuals of each type at a minimum. Finally, the panel facilitator must be well-trained and highly experienced in facilitating panels, as well as know the Enneagram in depth; otherwise, the panel facilitator will not know the best initial open-ended questions to ask each type panel or how to probe for more detailed and illuminating answers.

Typing interviews

Typing interviews involve an experienced Enneagram teacher interviewing another person and utilize specific, systematic questions that illuminate type. Interviews take between 45 minutes and 1.5 hours and may use questions that start with type 1 and end with type 9, or the questions may first focus on the three Centers of Intelligence, asking questions

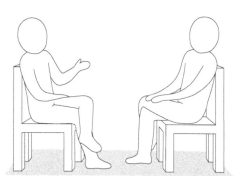

to identify the person's primary Center – Head, Heart or Body – and then move to which of the three types in this Center is the best fit. These are just two examples of interviewing formats; there are many others.

Because typing interviews are highly personalized, they can be very effective if the interviewer knows the Enneagram well, is adept at developing typing questions, and is an excellent listener. Interviewers need to listen not just for the words used, but also pay attention to the other person's body language, sentence construction, and more. I also use typing interviews in group settings, but I keep the questions non-invasive and seek to illuminate patterns rather than deeper psychological information.

Enneagram tests

There are five main Enneagram tests currently available, all of which are useful and have limitations when used in Enneagram typing. All five Enneagram tests also have validation and reliability studies to support their levels of accuracy, although they use different measures for this.

Most of the tests give percentages indicating the probability that the test-taker's highest score is his or her type. Most tests also report the test-taker's next highest scores and the percentage or likelihood that the second or third highest scoring types are the test-taker's actual type. The fact that typing-test results are typically not stated as 100% definitive shows integrity on the part of the test creators. If all Enneagram test-takers were highly self-aware, typing-test results would become increasingly more accurate. If Enneagram type were personality or character, measuring these qualities and assessing individuals against them would be much easier. But because Enneagram type is Ego structure, a far more complex phenomenon, Enneagram typing instruments are complex to construct.

This also means that if you are an Enneagram teacher, trainer or coach who relies *solely* on the test to determine type and you don't know the system and types well yourself, you won't be able to help another person sort out the test results for accuracy. In addition, a test-taker, even if the type score is accurate, only learns his or her type, not the other eight types or the system as a whole. For these reasons, it is best to not rely *solely* (emphasis on the word *solely*) on tests for accurate typing.

COMMONLY USED ENNEAGRAM TESTS

iEQ9 (Dirk Cloete) A series of questions to answer, with three different reports to choose from among – Mini, Standard, or Professional – and all test results are based on a smart algorithm so that as you answer the questions, the more precise the questions become; the newest test in the field (for purchase)

WEPSS (Jerry Wagner PhD) A series of questions to answer, with sufficient standardization, reliability, and validity to be included and favorably reviewed in Buros's Mental Measurements Yearbook – a respected authority in the test field – and a report with scores on the positive and negative features of your core type, plus more (for purchase)

RHETI (The Enneagram Institute) A series of forced-choice questions with paired statements, plus a profile report; the most used Enneagram test that has been available for several decades; the long version of the RHETI is far more accurate than the short version (for purchase)

Essential Enneagram Test (David Daniels MD) A set of nine paragraphs to choose from among, each paragraph describing a different type, with a report; test is also available in the book, *The Essential Enneagram* (for purchase)

EclecticEnergies.com (Ewald Berkers et al) An online test that sends an email of the test-taker's score, plus a description of that type; available in two versions (free)

APPENDIX B | 3 CENTERS OF INTELLIGENCE

There are many ways the concept of Centers of Intelligence is foundational to understanding the Enneagram system and the nine Enneagram types. First, a core purpose of the Enneagram is to become more whole, and one path to wholeness involves increasing our access to and productive use of each of the 3 Centers of Intelligence. Our Enneagram type provides a roadmap of insight into how each Enneagram type productively uses and misuses each of these 3 Centers. Even more, once you know your type accurately, the Enneagram offers precise type-based development activities for increasing access to each Center. Because of this, accurate typing is essential.

The second reason for understanding why the 3 Centers of Intelligence is important for accurate typing is that each Enneagram type is formed in one of the 3 Centers of Intelligence – the Head Center, the Heart Center, or the Body Center. This gives the Enneagram types formed in the same Center certain similarities because each Center has a specific human emotion connected with it. For the Head Center types (5, 6 and 7), the common emotion is fear, with three different sources of fear and ways of responding to it. For the Heart Center types (2, 3 and 4), the common emotion is sorrow, a sadness for creating an image that is not one's truest self. Each of the Heart Center types, however, creates a different kind of image. For the Body Center types (8, 9 and 1), the common emotion is anger, with three different ways of responding to anger. These three different ways of dealing with the same emotion can be useful in understanding how to identify one's type more accurately.

HEAD CENTER FUNCTIONS

Gather information | Generate ideas | Engage in mental processing | Rational analysis | Planning

PRODUCTIVE USES	Objective analysis	Astute insight	Productive planning
MISUSES	Overanalyzing	Projection	Overplanning

HEAD CENTER TYPES – *Five, Six, Seven*

Three Enneagram types formed in response to the emotion of fear

Fear of intrusion and depletion, and withdraw and depend solely on their own resources; gather abundant information to analyze for the purpose of developing preventive strategies

Most Common Misuse of Head Center: Overanalysis

Fear that what can go wrong will go wrong and that they and others are not up to the emergent challenges; create continuous anticipatory scenarios in order to overcome potential problems and/or go headlong into fearful situations to prove their own courage

Most Common Misuse of Head Center: Projection

Fear of restrictions, limitations, pain and discomfort; move away from fear by imagining positive future possibilities – also known as planning – and by generating exciting ideas rather than feeling uncomfortable or anxious

Most Common Misuse of Head Center: Overplanning

HEART CENTER OF INTELLIGENCE

HEART CENTER FUNCTIONS

Experience feelings | Relate to others emotionally | Sensitivity to the feelings and reactions of others

PRODUCTIVE USES	Empathy	Authentic relating	Compassion
MISUSES	Emotional manipulation	Playing roles	Oversensitivity

HEART CENTER TYPES – *Two, Three, Four*

Three Enneagram types that create an image, then experience sorrow for not being fully who they are

Create an image of being likeable, generous, and concerned for other people, then look to others for affirmation of their self-worth

Most Common Misuse of Heart Center: Emotional manipulation

Project an image of self-confidence, competence and success, then seek the respect and admiration of others for what they accomplish

Most Common Misuse of Heart Center: Playing roles

Create an image of being unique, special and different, then use their emotional sensitivity as a way to cover up not feeling good enough or deficient

Most Common Misuse of Heart Center: Oversensitivity

BODY CENTER FUNCTIONS

Movement | Experience physical sensations | Taking action or inaction | Control of one's environment

PRODUCTIVE USES	Taking effective action	Steadfastness	Gut knowing
MISUSES	Excessive action	Passivity	Reactivity

BODY CENTER TYPES – *Eight, Nine, One*

Three Enneagram types formed in response to the emotion of anger

Readily express anger, starting from the gut, and believe that anger is simply energy that needs release

Most Common Misuse of Body Center: Excessive action

Avoid their own anger and anger of others directed at them while mediating conflict among others to create harmony

Most Common Misuse of Body Center: Passivity

Manifest anger as resentment, irritation, frustration or continual small eruptions; believe anger is a negative emotion that must be kept under control

Most Common Misuse of Body Center: Reactivity

APPENDIX C | WINGS AND ARROWS

——————— ENNEAGRAM *WINGS* ———————

Wings are the Enneagram types on each side of your actual Enneagram type. These are secondary types of your core type, which means that you may also display some of the characteristics of these Enneagram types. Wings do not fundamentally change your Enneagram type; they merely add additional qualities. As can be seen on the Enneagram symbol, 9 and 2 are wings for 1s, 1 and 3 are wings for 2s, 2 and 4 are wings for 3s, and so forth.

You may have one wing, two wings, or no wings at all. It is also common to have had one wing be more active when you were younger and to have had another appear as you matured. People of the same Enneagram type and identical wings may use their wing qualities differently. However, the general wing descriptions for all nine Enneagram types given here may serve as guidelines to help you explore this aspect of the Enneagram.

——————— ENNEAGRAM *ARROWS* ———————

Arrow lines refer to the two types on the Enneagram symbol that have arrows pointing away from or toward your core Enneagram type, and you may show some characteristics of one or both of these two additional types. Access to your arrow lines can be beneficial to you, adding complexity, nuance, and flexibility, but they do not change your fundamental type – that is, your patterns of thinking, feeling, and behaving and your motivational structure remain the same. You may have strong links to one arrow number, both arrow numbers, or neither arrow number. People of the same Enneagram type who have links to their arrow numbers may use these arrow qualities quite differently.

Enneagram Fives

WINGS FOR FIVES

Four Wing: 5s with a 4 wing are more emotionally sensitive and expressive and also have an aesthetic perspective, perhaps engaging in the arts themselves – for example, writing poetry, novels, or screenplays and/or being photographers or artists.

Six Wing: 5s with a 6 wing emphasize and engage more readily with teams, tend to place greater value on loyalty, and may have enhanced intuitive insight. Although many 5s are insightful, their insights come more from putting facts together and engaging in extensive analysis. When 5s have a 6 wing, the insights come more quickly as the product of instantaneous processing.

ARROW LINES FOR FIVES

Arrow Line to Seven: 5s with strong access to arrow line 7 can be playful and spontaneous, far more comfortable being in highly visible roles (as if they are actors playing a particular part) and more highly engaged during social interactions.

Arrow Line from Eight: 5s with strong access to arrow line 8 display more depth of personal power, are less hesitant and more risk-taking and courageous, and move to action far more quickly.

Enneagram Sixes

WINGS FOR SIXES

Five Wing: When 6s have a 5 wing, they are more internally than externally focused and are also more self-contained and restrained, thus tempering their tendency to be reactive. In addition, they have an increased passion for knowledge and use the pursuit of knowledge not only to gather information in order to feel prepared, but also for the pure enjoyment of learning.

Seven Wing: It is sometimes said that 6s see the glass as half empty and 7s see it as half full. Thus, when 6s have a 7 wing, they see the whole glass and therefore tend to be more cheerful, less worried, more optimistic, and higher-energy.

ARROW LINES FOR SIXES

Arrow Line to Three: 6s with access to their 3 arrow can bypass their uncertainty by focusing on concrete goals and approaching their work with palpable confidence.

Arrow Line from Nine: 6s use their connection to 9 to relax, something very helpful to the normally tightly wired 6. For example, taking time to walk or enjoy nature fills 6s with a feeling of safety and calmness. They are more appreciative of different viewpoints and perspectives, a quality that can be invaluable in times of duress when 6s' start projecting and imagining their perspective is the only viable one.

Enneagram Sevens

WINGS FOR SEVENS

Six Wing: 7s with a 6 wing add the capacity to understand situations as being both half-full and half-empty. Because these 7s have an increased perceptiveness and an ability to anticipate potential problems, their actions become more deliberate and less based on their instantaneous reactions.

Eight Wing: 7s with an 8 wing tend to be more direct, assertive, and powerful. They have a more grounded presence and an increased desire to put ideas into action.

ARROW LINES FOR SEVENS

Arrow Line to One: When 7s have access to arrow line 1, their sense of responsibility and ability to focus increases, as does their precision and attention to detail. Although some 7s use these qualities on an ongoing basis, many display these most often as work deadlines approach.

Arrow Line from Five: 7s expend vast amounts of energy, and they eventually become fatigued. Access to 5 allows them to take time for themselves without engaging with others (although this may last only a few hours every few months). In addition, some 7s who have an extremely strong link to 5 enjoy quietude on a more regular basis, engage in self-reflection more often, and tend to be more self-contained.

Enneagram Twos

WINGS FOR TWOS

One Wing: When 2s have access to their 1 wing, they balance their focus on people with a dedication to task, are more discerning about situations and people, pay more attention to detail, and have an increased ability to be firm and to say *no*, with far less worry about how others will react to them when they assert themselves in this way.

Three Wing: 2s with a 3 wing are far more comfortable being visible, such as holding a high-profile leadership position. In addition, these 2s feel more comfortable acknowledging their desire to be successful; in fact, they often pursue being respected almost as much as being liked.

ARROW LINES FOR TWOS

Arrow Line to Eight: 2s with a strong link to 8 have a far deeper sense of their own personal power, tend to be bolder and more candid, and are more in touch with their energy and the power of their anger.

Arrow Line from Four: 2s who are strongly connected to type 4 have increased emotional depth because they focus on their own emotional reactions almost as much as on the feelings of others. They also tend to be more creative and original.

Enneagram Threes

WINGS FOR THREES

Two Wing: 3s with a 2 wing are far more sensitive to the feelings of others and more generous with their time and resources, and they often focus on helping others in their professional and/or personal lives.

Four Wing: 3s who have a 4 wing are far more in contact with their own feelings, are willing to engage in emotional conversations with others, have a deeper personal presence, and may engage in some form of artistic expression or refined level of artistic appreciation.

ARROW LINES FOR THREES

Arrow Line to Nine: When 3s have a strong connection to arrow line 9, they use this to relax, slow down their pace, and engage in activities simply for the pleasure of doing them. Being able to access type 9 also helps 3s to be more mellow and easygoing.

Arrow Line from Six: Although 3s can be smart, accessing their arrow line 6 augments their normal intelligence with an enhanced analytical capability and insightfulness. In addition, 3s with a link to type 6 tend to be more aware of their own true reactions rather than engaging in work as a way to avoid their feelings.

Enneagram Fours

WINGS FOR FOURS

Three Wing: When 4s have a 3 wing, they are more action-oriented, have higher and more consistent energy levels, exhibit more poise and confidence, and are more comfortable with being highly visible rather than shying away from visibility or feeling ambivalent about it.

Five Wing: 4s with a 5 wing are more objective and analytical, which provides a counterpoint to their more subjective emotional way of relating with others. In addition, they have an increased ability to perceive situations from a more considered and less reactive perspective and often demonstrate more self-restraint and self-containment.

ARROW LINES FOR FOURS

Arrow Line to Two: Because 4s normally focus on their own internal responses and personal experiences, a strong link to their arrow line 2 greatly enhances their attunement to other people. This increased attention to others helps these 4s be more responsive and more consistent in their interactions.

Arrow Line from One: When 4s have a strong connection to their arrow line 1, they become more objective and discerning of people and events, rather than making assessments based primarily on their emotional reactions. This provides them with greater balance, increased emotional and mental clarity, and enhanced attention to details.

Enneagram Eights

WINGS FOR EIGHTS

Seven Wing: 8s with a 7 wing add a lightheartedness to the usually more serious 8 outlook, are more high-spirited, and tend to be far more adventurous, willing to try new things in their personal and professional lives for the sake of experimentation and enjoyment.

Nine Wing: 8s with a 9 wing are interpersonally warmer, more calm, and less reactive, and they solicit and listen to others' opinions because they are more consensually oriented.

ARROW LINES FOR EIGHTS

Arrow Line to Five: 8s with a link to 5 often use the solitary qualities of 5 as a way to recharge themselves after particularly stressful or painful events or after expending their excessive mental, emotional, and physical energy to make big things happen. 8s with an extremely strong connection to 5 are often more highly self-reflective than other 8s, and they may engage in intellectual pursuits solely for the pleasure of learning.

Arrow Line from Two: 8s with a strong connection to 2 are warm, generous, and openhearted. They are more gentle than 8s without this link, and they show a deeper level of empathy for others.

Enneagram Nines

WINGS FOR NINES

Eight Wing: 9s with an 8 wing have a more take-charge orientation, exhibiting a solidity and forcefulness while still maintaining a desire to hear others' opinions. With a very strong 8 wing, 9s assert their own points of view more readily and make fast and clear decisions, even in the face of strong opposition.

One Wing: When 9s have a 1 wing, they are generally more attentive and alert – for example, they pay more attention to details and are more punctual and precise. Although 9s often diffuse their attention, a 1 wing increases their overall focus, acuity, clarity, and discernment.

ARROW LINES FOR NINES

Arrow Line to Six: When 9s have a strong link to 6, their level of insight about self, others, and situations increases, and they tend to be more deliberative and verbally expressive.

Arrow Line from Three: 9s with a strong connection to 3 have a stronger goal focus and results orientation, qualities that help them shift from the distractions of seeking comforting and comfortable activities to a more forward-moving, action-oriented approach to life and work.

Enneagram Ones

WINGS FOR ONES

Nine Wing: 1s with a 9 wing have a greater ability to relax and unwind without having to go on vacation, are less reactive when they disagree with someone, and are more likely to solicit the opinions of others rather than relying primarily on their own judgments or those of others whom they respect.

Two Wing: 1s with a 2 wing are more consistently generous and people-focused, in addition to being more gregarious and displaying more consistent warmth to others.

ARROW LINES FOR ONES

Arrow Line to Four: 1s who have a strong connection to type 4 pay more attention to their own inner experiences and are therefore more introspective and aware of their own feelings. In addition, a link to 4 adds originality and creativity to the ways in which 1s approach work, life, and any aesthetic interests they may have.

Arrow Line from Seven: 1s who have a strong connection to 7 are far more flexible, spontaneous, innovative, and lighthearted, and they have more fun.

APPENDIX D | 27 ENNEAGRAM SUBTYPES

Enneagram subtypes are an element that affects your Enneagram Ego structure. Enneagram subtypes are the way in which the emotional pattern – known as *passion* or *vice* – for each Enneagram type most frequently and intensely manifests in that person's behavior. Specifically, the subtype is formed from when the emotional pattern of the type combines with one of the three basic human instincts that is most active in the person: self-preservation, social, or one-to-one, also called intimacy or sexual.

3 BASIC INSTINCTS | *SELF-PRESERVATION, SOCIAL, AND ONE-TO-ONE*

To have one of these instincts more active in us does not necessarily mean we are good at getting our needs met in that arena or that we like that area of life. It means our attention and energy goes most consistently either toward that arena, away from it, or that we have the most ambivalence about that aspect of life. In many people, two of these instincts may be active, although these instincts may appear at different times in our lives or in different circumstances – for example, at home versus work.

Self-preservation instinct refers to issues of physical existence, safety, security, danger, resources, structure and control

Social instinct refers to issues of belonging, community, groups, social relationships, and influence

One-to-one instinct refers to issues about oneself in relation to one other person, affection, intimacy, bonding, attraction, and one-to-one relationships

PASSIONS **FOR EACH ENNEAGRAM TYPE**

The passion or vice for each Enneagram type is the emotional habit or pattern that fuels their emotional responses and when combined with the active basic instinct, generates subtype-specific behavioral responses.

TYPE 1 PASSION	*Anger*	Chronic anger and dissatisfaction with how things are
TYPE 2 PASSION	*Pride*	Inflated or deflated self-esteem based on doing for other people and the subsequent positive or negative reactions of others
TYPE 3 PASSION	*Deceit*	Feeling you must do everything possible to appear confident and successful, hiding parts of yourself that do not conform to this image
TYPE 4 PASSION	*Envy*	Consciously or unconsciously comparing yourself to others with resultant feelings of deficiency, superiority, or both
TYPE 5 PASSION	*Avarice*	An intense desire to guard everything related to oneself, combined with automatic detachment from feelings
TYPE 6 PASSION	*Fear*	Feelings of anxiety, deep concern, and panic that the worst will occur, that others cannot be trusted, and that you and they are not capable of meeting the challenges that present themselves
TYPE 7 PASSION	*Gluttony*	The insatiable, unrelenting thirst for new stimulation of all kinds: food, people, experience, ideas, excitement
TYPE 8 PASSION	*Lust*	Excessiveness in a variety of forms as a way to avoid and deny feelings of vulnerability and weakness
TYPE 9 PASSION	*Laziness*	A lethargy in paying attention to your own feelings, thoughts, and needs, thus disabling desired action

For each of the three subtypes of an Enneagram type, two of the subtypes move in the direction of the type's passion, and one of the subtypes – called the countertype – begins by moving in the direction of the passion, and then pulls back, at least to some extent. For this reason, the countertype of the type is the most likely of the three subtypes to be confused with another type, although other subtypes can also be confused with other types. The countertypes for each type are indicated below.

Three Subtypes for Ones | the passion of anger

Although all 1s seek perfection, avoid mistakes, and experience anger as chronic dissatisfaction and irritation with the many things in life and work that are not as they should be, there are three distinct ways in which 1s manifest *anger*.

SELF-PRESERVATION SUBTYPE 1 ("WORRY")* focus on getting everything structured and organized correctly, and experience anxiety, worry, and *anger* in the form of irritation and frustration when they think this may not or is not occurring. Wanting to make sure that everything is under control, they emphasize precision and extreme accuracy as a way to make certain that everything is done right, feeling *angry* with themselves or situations when this does not occur. *Can be confused with a 6 or self-preservation subtype 3*

SOCIAL SUBTYPE 1 ("NON-ADAPTABILITY") perceive themselves as role models who represent the right way of being and behaving. In their view, they set the standard for how to be and their *anger* arises when others do not respect them for this or do not live up to their example. Social subtype 1s also focus their efforts on correcting and perfecting social institutions, critiquing them and manifesting *anger* when social systems and structures do not measure up to expectation.

ONE-TO-ONE SUBTYPE 1 ("ZEAL")* have a driving need to perfect others, particularly those who matter to them, as well as to perfect society in general. They perceive reforming others as both their right and their responsibility, and they go about this with intensity, passion and *anger* when people and society do not meet their expectations. *This is the countertype and can be confused with one-to-one subtype 8.*

Three Subtypes for Twos | the passion of pride

All 2s have their sense of self-worth, personal *pride*, and importance integrally linked with how others respond to them, and they want to be viewed as appealing individuals who are valued for helping others and for being able to influence things in a positive direction. *Pride* can be thought of as an inflation or deflation of self-worth based on the reactions of others. As a result of this self-inflation, 2s can be thought of as perceiving themselves as Enneagram royalty, even 2s who may have suffered. There are three distinct ways in which 2s manifest *pride*.

SELF-PRESERVATION SUBTYPE 2 ("ME-FIRST/PRIVILEGE")* deny their own needs for protection while also trying to attract others who will provide exactly that for them. Drawing others to them in the same way that children do – that is, by being appealing and appearing to be without guile – self-preservation subtype 2s take *pride* in being able to do this and, at the same time, are also ambivalent about close relationships and less trusting than social subtype or one-to-one subtype 2s. Self-preservation subtype 2s are the princes and princesses, who give up the rights of adulthood for the privileges of childhood. **This is the countertype and can be confused with self-preservation subtype 6.*

SOCIAL SUBTYPE 2 ("AMBITION")* focus on helping groups more than individuals and are more intellectually oriented and comfortable being in visibly powerful positions than individuals of the other two subtype variations. Social subtype 2s are less concerned with how specific individuals respond to them and more focused on group-level reactions, which is a result of their desire to stand above the crowd in some way, feeling *pride* when this occurs. Social subtype 2s are the emperors and empresses, who feel they must continuously prove that they have earned the right to royalty through their actions on behalf of groups and systems, while appearing that they have not made a great effort to do so. **Can be confused with social subtype 8*

ONE-TO-ONE SUBTYPE 2 ("AGGRESSION/SEDUCTION")* are primarily oriented to individual relationships and meeting the needs of important people and partners. They take *pride* in being able to attract specific individuals as a way of getting their needs met – they feel they have value or worth when chosen by someone important – but they are also highly motivated to meet the needs of these individuals as a way of developing and sustaining the relationship. One-to-one subtype 2s, the kings and queens, own their royal status as a birthright, with little need to prove it or justify it other than by providing attention and support to key individuals in their lives. **Can be confused with one-to-one subtype 4*

All 3s feel they must appear successful in order to gain the admiration and respect of others, and they avoid failure in any form by hiding parts of themselves that do not conform to their image of success, deceiving not only others, but also themselves as they come to believe that the image they create is actually who they are. Thus, *deceit* starts first with self-deceit. There are three distinct ways in which 3s manifest *deceit*.

SELF-PRESERVATION SUBTYPE 3 ("SECURITY")* want to be seen as self-reliant, autonomous, and hardworking, thus portraying an image of being a good or ideal person. The self-preservation subtype 3 creates an image of having no image and, therefore, may not even perceive this as a form of deceit. *This is the countertype and can be confused with a 6 or self-preservation subtype 1.*

SOCIAL SUBTYPE 3 ("PRESTIGE")* manifest their *deceit* as a result of wanting to be seen as successful and admirable in the context of specific reference groups – that is, the groups in which they want to be admired and perceived as successful. To this end, social subtype 3s continuously try to bolster their image by not acknowledging or revealing aspects of themselves such as feelings of anxiety, not knowing how to do something, and more. They also like to be around other successful people, because this proximity reinforces both the social subtype 3's image and status. *Can be confused with a 7*

ONE-TO-ONE SUBTYPE 3 ("MASCULINITY/FEMININITY")* want to be viewed as successful by people who are very important to them, primarily by appearing attractive to these people in some way, but also by helping these people achieve success. Their *deceit* comes in the form of not acknowledging parts of themselves, or not showing aspects of themselves, that might not be attractive to these others. *Can be confused with one-to-one subtype 2*

Three Subtypes for Fours / the passion of envy

All 4s desire a feeling of deep connection both with their own interior worlds and with other people as a way to avoid feeling deficient or not good enough. Because they believe there is something lacking within them – although they cannot define exactly what this is – 4s consciously and unconsciously compare themselves to others. This process of comparing oneself to others, called *envy*, results in 4s feeling deficient, superior or both. The three subtypes of 4 look quite different from each other.

SELF-PRESERVATION SUBTYPE 4 ("RECKLESS/DAUNTLESS")* try to bear their suffering in silence as a way to prove that they are good enough by virtue of enduring inner anguish. In addition, they engage in nonstop activity and/or reckless behavior as a way to feel excited and energized and to avoid not feeling as good as others. Of all three subtypes of type 4, self-preservation subtype 4s do not appear to be as *envious* as the other two subtypes of 4. However, their constant comparisons – envy – are more subsurface. *This is the countertype and can be confused with a 7 or a 3.*

SOCIAL SUBTYPE 4 ("SHAME") focus more on their deficiencies and also on earning the understanding and appreciation of the groups to which they belong. They want understanding and appreciation for their suffering and sorrows, and desire acknowledgment for their heartfelt contributions to groups, while at the same time they often feel marginal to or not fully part of groups. Social subtype 4s are usually more aware of their *envy* – that is, their continuous comparisons of self to others.

ONE-TO-ONE SUBTYPE 4 ("COMPETITION")* feel compelled to express their needs and feelings outwardly and can be highly competitive with others to gain attention, to be heard, and to be acknowledged for their perspectives and accomplishments. Winning is perceived as another avenue for being understood, and coming out on top is seen as a way to resolve their continuous comparisons – *envy* – with others. *Can be confused with one-to-one subtype 8*

Three Subtypes for Fives | the passion of avarice

All 5s have an intense need to acquire knowledge and wisdom and a similarly strong desire to avoid intrusion and loss of energy, and they guard and preserve everything that they think they will need – for example, information, physical space, emotional privacy, personal energy, and resources. There are three distinct ways in which 5s manifest the above, which is called *avarice*. The three subtypes of 5 look very similar to one another.

SELF-PRESERVATION SUBTYPE 5 ("CASTLE") are primarily concerned with being intruded upon and being overextended physically and energetically. In a sense, they hoard their involvement with others in the same way they are *avaricious* about their scarce resources.

SOCIAL SUBTYPE 5 ("TOTEM") want to find and develop strong connections with individuals and groups who share their super-ideals, but they become disengaged when forced to live in a way that is not aligned with these higher-order beliefs. They focus on the group in search of extraordinary individuals, then are *avaricious* about these relationships, their shared ideals and, in the 5's view, their superior values.

ONE-TO-ONE SUBTYPE 5 ("CONFIDENCE")* search for a strong, deep connection with one other person whom they can trust and share confidences with, then are *avaricious* about what they share with people other than this special individual. They are also *avaricious* with regard to sharing this other person or any special relationships with others. **This is the countertype, although it does not usually get confused with another type.*

Three Subtypes for Sixes / the passion of fear

All 6s seek meaning, certainty, and trust, hoping that the best is possible, yet simultaneously feeling *fear* that this will not happen, and they doubt that others are trustworthy and/or whether they themselves are capable of meeting the challenges involved. There are three distinct ways in which 6s manifest *fear*. The one-to-one subtype 6 looks dramatically different from the other two subtypes.

SELF-PRESERVATION SUBTYPE 6 ("WARMTH")* manifest *fear* as an intense need to feel protected from danger, often seeking the family or a surrogate family to provide this. Self-preservation subtype 6s also use warmth and friendliness as a way to attract and maintain these types of support groups for the purpose of making themselves feel safe. *Can be confused with self-preservation subtype 2*

SOCIAL SUBTYPE 6 ("DUTY")* deal with *fear* by focusing on the rules, regulations, and prescribed ways of behaving within their environment in an attempt to keep their own behavior in the acceptable range, trying to make sure they do nothing that will cause authority figures to chastise or punish them for going astray. *Can be confused with a 1*

ONE-TO-ONE SUBTYPE 6 ("STRENGTH/BEAUTY")* are generally the most counterphobic. They express their *fear* primarily through the denial of their anxieties and vulnerabilities by pushing against the *fear*, appearing bold, confident, and sometimes fierce. They can also engage in physical or verbal behavior that makes them feel and appear highly courageous. This can be thought of as anti-fear generated by the avoidance of *fear*. *This is the countertype and can be confused with an 8.*

All 7s have an insatiable thirst or *gluttony* for new stimulation of all kinds and distract themselves with interesting people, ideas, and pleasurable experiences, which allows them to avoid their fear of painful emotions and difficult situations. There are three distinct ways in which 7s manifest *gluttony*.

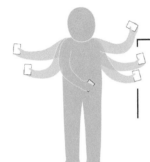

SELF-PRESERVATION SUBTYPE 7 ("KEEPERS OF THE CASTLE") are *gluttonous* about creating close networks of family, friends, and colleagues, not only to keep themselves feeling both stimulated and secure but also to generate new and interesting opportunities to pursue.

SOCIAL SUBTYPE 7 ("SACRIFICE")* sacrifice some of their *gluttonous* needs for stimulation in service of the group or of some ideal that is extremely important to them. At the same time, they are aware of wanting to pursue their desires, but choose to postpone them momentarily and want to be explicitly thanked or acknowledged for this sacrifice. They do, however, then pursue and satisfy their desires later on. **This is the countertype and can be confused with a 2.*

ONE-TO-ONE SUBTYPE 7 ("SUGGESTIBILITY/FASCINATION") are dreamers, with a need to see the stark reality of the world through rose-colored glasses, and they are the most optimistic of the three subtypes of type 7. Often, they become fascinated with one other person, become satiated with that person over time, then find someone new who intrigues and stimulates them. Their *gluttony* is in the form of romantic, idealized dreaming.

Three Subtypes for Eights | the passion of lust

As a way to pursue justice and control and to avoid and deny their anxiety and sadness or feelings of vulnerability, 8s engage in a variety of self-satisfying behaviors and do these in an excessive way, which is called *lust*; for example, they take big and immediate action, work superhuman hours, eat too much food, exercise for three hours a day for a week and then don't exercise for two months, and more. There are three distinct ways in which 8s manifest *lust*.

SELF-PRESERVATION SUBTYPE 8 ("SURVIVAL") focus their excessiveness or *lust* on getting what they need for survival, and they become highly frustrated, intolerant, and angry when the fulfillment of these needs is thwarted. Of the three 8 subtypes, the self-preservation subtype 8s tend to speak the least and to approach situations – particularly those they deem important to their survival – in a highly strategic way that allows them to get the upper hand.

SOCIAL SUBTYPE 8 ("SOLIDARITY")* vigorously protect others from unjust and unfair authorities and systems and challenge social norms. At the same time, they seek power, influence, and pleasure. Wanting loyalty from others and being highly loyal themselves, they derive a feeling of power from challenging others as well as from defending those under their protection, which makes them feel less vulnerable. Their *lust* is in the form of excessiveness for groups and causes where they become central to them, often organizing or leading them. *This is the countertype and can be confused with social subtype 2.*

ONE-TO-ONE SUBTYPE 8 ("POSSESSION")* are the most intense, rebellious, and emotional of the three subtypes of 8. Provocative and passionate in a way that draws others toward them, these 8s derive their power and influence from being at the center of things, from the strong and energetic connections they develop, and from the fervent way in which they express their positions and values. They are *lustful* and possessive of those with whom they are intimate or close. *Can be confused with one-to-one subtype 4 or one-to-one subtype 6*

In order to maintain harmony and comfort and to avoid conflict, 9s numb themselves to their own reactions by becoming lethargic – also called *laziness* – and by not paying attention to their own deeper feelings, needs, and impulses. This self-numbing disables them from knowing what they think, feel and want, and from knowing what action is the right one to take. There are three distinct ways in which 9s manifest *laziness*.

SELF-PRESERVATION SUBTYPE 9 ("APPETITE") use the comfort of merging with routines, as well as rhythmic and pleasant activities, as a way of not paying attention to themselves. This form of *laziness* about self distracts them from important priorities, conflict, and distress. Many self-preservation subtype 9s also acquire and then merge with items they collect – for example, books, stamps, magnets, ceramic figures – and their desire for these objects increases the more they obtain.

SOCIAL SUBTYPE 9 ("PARTICIPATION")* work extremely hard on behalf of a group, organization, or cause that they support or belong to as a way of not focusing on themselves; thus, they use working hard and merging with a group as their form of *laziness* about self. Social subtype 9s are usually very friendly, and their need to feel a part of things is rooted in their underlying feeling of not fitting in. Thus, social subtype 9s lose their sense of self in the service of others, rarely showing the pain, stress, and overwork they experience as a result. **This is the countertype and can be confused with a 3.*

ONE-TO-ONE SUBTYPE 9 ("FUSION/UNION")* join or merge with others who are important to them as a way of not paying attention to their own thoughts, feelings, and needs. This fusion with others results in one-to-one subtype 9s becoming disconnected from their own deep desires and confusing their own sense of fulfillment with the desires and gratification of those with whom they have merged. In this way, they use fusion with specific others as their form of *laziness* about self. **Can be confused with a 2*

APPENDIX E | ENNEAGRAM TRIADS

There are several groupings of three on the Enneagram, one of which is particularly useful in typing: the *optimistic* triad (7, 9 and 2), the *intensity* triad (4, 6 and 8), and the *competency* triad (1, 3 and 5).

Optimistic Triad | TYPES 7, 9 AND 2

The three types in the optimistic triad, also called the positive outlook triad, have a positive overlay on reality so that the world looks better than it actually is. 7s are the most optimistic, taking a positive view of just about everything. 9s are moderately positive, perceiving people and events as generally pleasurable. Finally, 2s want and try to see the best in other people – that is, until they don't! Although the three types within this triad are very different, people often get confused between and among them.

Intensity Triad
TYPES 4, 6 AND 8

Types 4, 6 and 8 are the most intense of the nine Enneagram types. Their intensity, however, comes from different sources. The 4s' intensity is emotional, a result of so many feelings playing and replaying inside them and their drive for intense, authentic interactions. The 6s' intensity is the result of their ever-active minds playing and replaying various scenarios. The 8s' intensity is more somatic and comes from the body. It is often noted that people can feel the intense presence of 8s, even when 8s are saying absolutely nothing. Intensity is a very strong energy that these three types share, so that discerning the source of the intensity can be a key factor in differentiating between and among these types.

Competency Triad
TYPES 1, 3 AND 5

These three types want to both experience themselves as highly competent and want to be treated by others as highly competent, although competency has a different meaning to each of these types. For 1s, competency means being right, knowing how to organize in the best way, and having the most correct opinion. For 3s, competency means knowing how and being able to move things forward, being able to get great results, and understanding something that they think they should know. For 5s, competency means being capable in terms of their depth and breadth of knowledge and understanding how things fit together. An exploration of what competency means helps sort out which of these three types is the best fit.

ADDITIONAL RESOURCES

While there are many excellent Enneagram resources available, these specifically relate to typing skills.

BOOKS

Enneagram Overview

Nine Lenses on the World by Jerry Wagner PhD
Offers a robust psychological perspective on the Enneagram and the 9 types

The Complete Enneagram by Beatrice Chestnut PhD
Offers full descriptions of the 27 Enneagram subtypes

The Wisdom of the Enneagram by Don Riso and Russ Hudson
Offers the Levels of Development for each type to help differentiate why people of the same type may be so different from one another

Essential Enneagram by David Daniels MD and Virginia Price PhD
An easy-to-read psychological overview of the 9 types

Enneagram in Action

Bringing Out the Best in Yourself at Work by Ginger Lapid-Bogda PhD
Describes the 9 types in action in a variety of contexts: feedback, conflict, communication, leadership, teams

What Type of Leader Are You? by Ginger Lapid-Bogda PhD
Describes the 9 types in action in specific leadership competencies

Bringing Out the Best in Everyone You Coach by Ginger Lapid-Bogda PhD
Features 9 chapters that probe deeply into the Ego-structure elements of each type

Spiritual Enneagram

Spiritual Dimensions of the Enneagram by Sandra Maitri
A robust explanation of the spiritual aspects of each type, with a focus on the Holy Ideas, the higher mental state for each type

Enneagram Information

Selected websites offering a breadth and depth of free and accurate Enneagram information:

TheEnneagramInBusiness.com
The site of Ginger Lapid-Bogda, providing information about the Enneagram system and types as well as the business applications

Integrative9.com
The site of Integrative Enneagram Solutions (Dirk Cloete)

EnneagramWorldwide.com
The site of the Enneagram in the Narrative Tradition (Helen Palmer-David Daniels), providing information about the Enneagram system and types

TheEnneagramAtWork.com
The site of Peter O'Hanrahan, providing information about the Enneagram system, types and personal and professional applications

EnneagramSpectrum.com
The site of Jerry Wagner, providing information about the Enneagram system, theory, types and applications

EnneagramInstitute.com
The site of Russ Hudson and the late Don Riso, providing information about the system, types, and relationships between types

Conscious.tv
A site with a robust Enneagram section, providing excellent Enneagram type panels, 3-5 people of the same type being interviewed by Iain McNay or Renate McNay

TYPING AIDS

Enneagram Tests (see Appendix A for descriptions of these tests)

iEQ9 | Integrative Enneagram Solutions | *Integrative9.com*

RHETI | *EnneagramInstitute.com*

WEPSS | *EnneagramSpectrum.com*

Essential Enneagram | *EnneagramWorldwide.com*

Eclectic Energies | *EclecticEnergies.com*

Enneagram Apps

Know Your Type | *EnneagramApp.com*
Available on iOS (Apple), Google Play (Android) and Kindle Fire (Amazon); contains an animated typing card section as well as an array of other interactive Enneagram information

Training Tools

TheEnneagramInBusiness.com
Offers 27 trainings tools, three of which are specifically focused on typing: Enneagram Typing Cards, Enneagram Workbook, Enneagram Discovery Deck, plus one on Levels of Self-Mastery that focuses on the different self-mastery levels within type

TRAINING PROGRAMS FOR TYPING

The following programs specifically teach typing skills:

The Enneagram in Business | *TheEnneagramInBusiness.com*
Specific programs that have typing components: *Bringing Out the Best in Yourself at Work*; *What Type of Leader Are You?*; *Bringing Out the Best in Everyone You Coach*; and *The Art of Typing*

Enneagram Worldwide | *EnneagramWorldwide.com*
Offers long-term programs that also include typing skills, as well as specialized typing skills programs

Enneagram Institute | *EnneagramInstitute.com*
Offers long-term programs that also include typing skills

Integrative Enneagram Solutions | *Integrative9.com*
Offers short programs that train practitioners how to use iEQ9 test

The Enneagram in Business | who we are

The Enneagram in Business is dedicated to increasing consciousness worldwide using the Enneagram, often integrated with other approaches, to increase both capability and possibility at the individual, leadership, team, organizational and community levels. We provide best-in-class resources needed to bring the Enneagram to organizations, including professional services for companies, professional certificate programs for trainers, coaches and consultants, engaging training tools, and online and app-based learning platforms.

With a network of over 70 Enneagram professionals worldwide, we work in organizations of all sizes from various industries, including for-profit, non-profit, professional service organizations and government agencies. We adhere to Blue Ocean ethical standards of practice and values, including honesty, respect for intellectual property, open source sharing, collaboration, fair pricing, and client focus.

Enneagram books by Ginger Lapid-Bogda PhD

Bringing Out the Best in Yourself at Work (2004) | core work applications of the Enneagram

What Type of Leader Are You? (2007) | develop leadership competencies using the Enneagram

Bringing Out the Best in Everyone You Coach (2010) | high-impact coaching using the Enneagram

The Enneagram Development Guide (2011) | 50+ powerful development activities for each Enneagram type

Consulting with the Enneagram (2015) | a systematic structure for achieving powerful results with clients

The Enneagram Coloring Book (2016) | a right and left-brained way to learn the Enneagram

The Art of Typing (2018) | powerful tools for Enneagram typing

Author

GINGER LAPID-BOGDA PHD

Ginger Lapid-Bogda, an internationally recognized Enneagram author, trainer, keynote speaker, OD consultant and coach, is considered a world leader in bringing the insights of the Enneagram to organizations across the globe. Author of seven Enneagram books, she offers organization development consulting, training, and in depth coaching; five global professional certification programs; 29 training tools; and the comprehensive Enneagram app, "Know Your Type." She is past president of the International Enneagram Association and founder of the Enneagram in Business Network. You can find more information on her website, **theenneagraminbusiness.com**.
Contact: **info@theenneagraminbusiness.com**

Illustrator

SUENAON

Suenaon (real name is Noa-Neus Fuentes Romero) is an illustrator and graphic designer from Galicia, Spain with more than 8 years of experience in this sector. Her professional career was developed in Barcelona, were she grew up as an artist. She specializes in hand and digital drawing, marketing materials design, photo retouching and editorial layout. Noa-Neus is currently living in the US, enhancing her skills and enjoying Southern California. You can find more information on her website, **suenaon.com**.
Contact: **hola@suenaon.com**

THE ART OF TYPING
POWERFUL TOOLS FOR ENNEAGRAM TYPING

" I've found it useful to explore an issue related to the distinctive ways in which two types can look alike. For example, in typing a person uncertain whether he was a 1 or a 6, I said, "1s are sometimes wrong but rarely in doubt; 6s are often right but rarely without doubt." "Oh, I see," he said, "I'm a 6!"

Judith Searle, an actress, writer, and internationally respected Enneagram teacher, is the author of *The Literary Enneagram* and co-author of *Sex, Love and Your Personality: The Nine Faces of Intimacy*

"

" I would start by asking the person what they value, what they are passionate about. For example, 5s like to learn; 1s like to make things and people better; 2s enjoy loving and supporting, etc.

Jerry Wagner PhD is the creator of the WEPSS Enneagram assessment, author of numerous Enneagram books including *Nine Lenses on the World*, and honorary founder of the International Enneagram Association

" When starting the journey to discover type, be gentle with yourself and allow type to unfold. Be willing to not know for a period of time and simply observe your patterns and habits of mind. Take time to observe with the inner witness, not the inner critic. Not just the behaviors but the motivations of why you do what you do.

Tracy Tresidder, Enneagram teacher, coach, trainer and consultant, also works with teenagers and families and is co-author of *Knowing Me: Knowing Them; Understanding Your Parenting Personality by Discovering the Enneagram*

The Enneagram In Business Press
Santa Monica, California | 310.829.3309

www.TheEnneagramInBusiness.com

CPSIA information can be obtained
at www.ICGtesting.com
Printed in the USA
BVHW021032060321
601619BV00001B/11

9 780996 344777